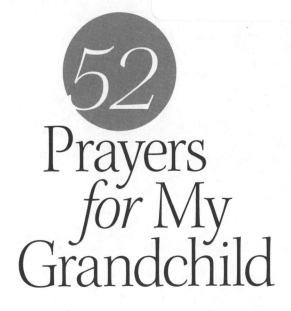

52 Prayers *for* My Grandchild

Steve & Annie CHAPMAN

HARVEST HOUSE PUBLISHERS
EUGENE, OREGON

Scripture quotations and biblical references are from these versions:

The Holy Bible, New International Version®, NIV®. Copyright © 1973, 1978, 1984, 2011 by Biblica, Inc.® Used by permission. All rights reserved worldwide.

The New American Standard Bible ®, © 1960, 1962, 1963, 1968, 1971, 1972, 1973, 1975, 1977, 1995 by The Lockman Foundation. Used by permission. (www.Lockman.org)

The ESV® Bible (The Holy Bible, English Standard Version®), copyright © 2001 by Crossway, a publishing ministry of Good News Publishers. Used by permission. All rights reserved.

The *Holy Bible*, New Living Translation, copyright © 1996, 2004, 2007, 2013 by Tyndale House Foundation. Used by permission of Tyndale House Publishers, Inc., Carol Stream, Illinois 60188. All rights reserved.

The Message. Copyright © by Eugene H. Peterson 1993, 1994, 1995, 1996, 2000, 2001, 2002. Used by permission of Tyndale House Publishers, Inc.

Cover design by Koechel Peterson & Associates, Minneapolis, Minnesota

Cover photo © Maria Teijeiro / Thinkstock

52 PRAYERS FOR MY GRANDCHILD
Copyright © 2015 Steve and Annie Chapman
Published by Harvest House Publishers
Eugene, Oregon 97402
www.harvesthousepublishers.com

Library of Congress Cataloging-in-Publication Data
Chapman, Steve.
    52 prayers for my grandchild / Steve and Annie Chapman.
        pages cm
    ISBN 978-0-7369-5314-6 (pbk.)
    ISBN 978-0-7369-5315-3 (eBook)
    1. Grandparents—Religious life. 2. Grandparenting—Religious aspects—Christianity. 3. Grandparents—Prayers and devotions. I. Title. II. Title: Fifty-two prayers for my grandchild.
    BV4528.5.C43 2015
    242'.845—dc23
                                                                          2014038258

Printed in the United States of America

15 16 17 18 19 20 21 22 23 / BP-JH / 10 9 8 7 6 5 4 3 2 1

To our treasures, who
joined our family in this order:
Lily Anne
Josephine Tish
Sylvia Grace
Nathalie Margaret
Williamson George

We also extend this dedication to any
grands and great-grands who might come later.

Acknowledgments

We'd like to say thank-you to…

- *our children and their spouses* for providing the joy of the grandchildren who have blessed our home.
- *our parents* who taught us that the role of a parent is to leave a good legacy while a grandparent leaves good memories.
- *our grandchildren* for the way they make our hearts smile.
- *the Harvest House Publishers staff* for inviting us to make public the hopes and prayers we have for our grandchildren.
- *Ed and Sharon Ditto* for the use of their beautiful and peace-filled cabin in the hills of Tennessee where much of this book was written.

A Grandparent's Prayer

Thank You, Lord, I've seen my children's children,
Heaven's love in flesh and bone.
Oh, how sweet it is to hear them laughing
Where it's been quiet far too long.

Lord, I pray for these treasures
You have given to my years.
Until they meet You in forever
Take their hand and keep them near.

Lord, I pray when they get older
And my name comes to their minds,
May it be the one thing they remember—
They saw Your blessed face in mine.[1]

A Note from Steve and Annie

Annie and I are musicians who travel the United States sharing the importance of faith and family. When our son, Nathan, and daughter, Heidi, were very young, they traveled with us. On one trip to the state of Texas, we stopped in to see some friends who lived in Houston. While we visited in their kitchen, Nathan, who was around five years old at the time, found his way to the backyard and began to explore the premises.

As we enjoyed the conversation with our friends, I could see Nathan through the kitchen window. I felt relieved that he was free of the confines of our van and could stretch his little legs. Suddenly I saw something that made me nearly choke on my ice water. I jumped up abruptly and ran to the back door. I had to get to my little boy!

Without knowing what pain lurked in the dome-shaped mound just a foot or two from him, Nathan was approaching a nest of fire ants. To him, the sandy mound looked like a small mountain of fun to play in. To me, it looked like major trouble.

I opened the door of the house and ran toward Nathan. At the last second before he reached for the pile of dirt, I scooped up my little guy and headed to the patio. If I'd waited just a few more ticks of the clock, Nathan would have been covered with angry ants that would have inflicted the kind of pain no one wants to suffer.

Recently Annie and I talked about the incident and what terrible pain our son could have experienced in that Texas backyard all those years ago. It still makes us shudder to imagine the amount of poisonous venom that would have been injected into his tender skin. We're utterly grateful that one of us was there for him and saw the impending danger he faced so disaster could be avoided.

Today, we have grandchildren who are, so to speak, exploring the backyard of today's world. From the vantage point of our "window of life experience," we recognize many of the dangers that threaten them. While we're not their parents, we're aware that we have the God-ordained privilege of being watchful in prayer over our grandchildren by going to Him on behalf of their spiritual, emotional, and physical well-being.

We're glad you're joining us on this enjoyable and important journey. These prayers are products of our sincere desire that our grandchildren (and yours!) will "in all respects…prosper and be in good health, just as [their] soul prospers" (3 John 2). We hope you'll pray these powerful, biblically based words over your grandchildren for a long time.

Before we get started in praying for our grandchildren, we hope you'll unite with us as we pray…

Grandparents' Prayer

As grandparents, we humbly and fully submit ourselves to You, heavenly Father. We ask You to create in us clean hearts and renew a right spirit within us. Give us clean hands and pure hearts so when we approach Your throne on behalf of our grandchildren, we'll find Your mercy and grace in time of need. Please grant us the strength to throw off everything that hinders and the sin that so easily entangles us. Help us daily fix our eyes on Jesus, the author and perfecter of our faith.

We come near to You because You promised You would come near to us. It's wonderful to be close to You. We've made You, sovereign Lord, our refuge. And we'll tell our grandchildren of Your deeds.

On our own, we're unworthy of Your listening ear, but You tell us that in our weakness Your power is made perfect and we're made stronger in You. Not by our might nor by our power is this done, but by Your Spirit.

Father, we trust in You with all our hearts and do not depend on our own understanding, but we'll seek Your will in all we do. We pray that You'll show us which paths to take. Only as we follow You and depend on Your strength will we be in the best position to bring our grandchildren to You in prayer.

We know You're able to do for our grandchildren far more abundantly than all we could ask or even think about. We're relying on Your power at work within us and within them.

We praise You, God. We won't forget Your benefits. Thank You for forgiving our sins through Your Son, Jesus Christ. You heal our diseases and redeem our lives from the pit. You crown us with love and compassion. We're grateful that You're compassionate and gracious, slow to anger, and abounding in love. You require clean hands and a pure heart, and we find comfort knowing that with Your cleansing and refining fire at work within us, we can stand before You.

Thank You for hearing and answering our prayers.

In Jesus' name we pray, amen.

Psalm 51:10; Psalm 24:3-4; Hebrews 4:16; Hebrews 12:1-2; Hebrews 12:2; James 4:8; 2 Corinthians 12:9; Zechariah 4:6; Proverbs 3:5-6; Ephesians 3:20-21; Psalm 103:1-8; Psalm 24:4; Hebrews 10:19-22

1

Discovering Jesus

I pray that my grandchildren
will make wise choices.

A New Option

Our days are made up of a series of choices. We choose if and when
to get out of bed in the morning…or afternoon. We choose to put on
clothes, or perhaps it's a day when we choose to stay in our jammies.
Our choice. We choose what and how much we're going to eat for
breakfast. When we reach for the doughnut with the chocolate sprin-
kles and wash it down with 24 ounces of Red Bull, we're choosing what
kind of health we want and what our appearance will be like in a year.

We choose to go to work or goof off. We do our work or don't do our
work. Throughout the day we encounter choice after choice…until it's
time to go to bed—and that's another choice. The amount of sleep we
get helps determine what the next day will be like.

While many of our choices may seem relatively unimportant,
there are some that have generational and even eternal consequences. I
(Annie) am thinking about one choice in particular that was made by
Steve's parents that forever changed the Chapman spiritual family tree.

P.J. and Lillian Chapman made a lot of choices in their young lives.
As a dating couple, they frequented juke joints and honky-tonks on the
weekends. They chose to jitterbug their evenings away at the Ritzy Ray,
a local nightlife magnet on the outskirts of their little town. Before long,
they chose to elope. Eventually, they chose to settle down and have a
family—a daughter and a son.

P.J. and Lillian were exploring ideas for bettering their struggling financial situation, when Lillian came up with an idea. She decided she needed to get more education so she could qualify for better-paying work. But what interrupted her plan resulted in an even more important and lasting choice.

Many years later, their son, Steve, a songwriter and musician, enlisted the help of his friend Dana Bacon to create a song that explains what happened that fateful day way back in 1949. Steve and I shared this song with our grandchildren, and we continue to share it with our audiences (and you) as an encouragement.

I Didn't Make It Down to Logan

From the last house in the hollow,
Up on Godby Branch,
She walked out the dirt road
On her way to take a chance
That night school down in Logan
Seemed like the only way.
They needed more to feed a family
Than just a taxi driver's pay.

Her young husband kept the baby;
She'd be back at ten.
But it was quarter past eleven
When she came walkin' in.
He said, "How'd things go at class tonight?"
She said, "I don't know…
Before I made it to the bus stop,
Jesus saved my soul."

"I heard singin' comin' from the church on the hill,
Sweetest sound I ever heard…breakin' down my will.
I could feel it—the Spirit—callin' out to me.
Now I believe…and that's why
I didn't make it down to Logan tonight."

He said, "I know you'd make a good nurse,
But did you change your mind?
We could really use the money
To help us make it through these times.
And, girl, it sure sounds crazy
To hear you say you're born again."
She said, "If you'll just go there with me,
I know you'll understand."

It was only two nights later,
he went with her down that road.
And when my mama tells the story—
the part I love the most…

"I heard singin' comin' from the church on the hill,
Sweetest sound I ever heard…breakin' down my will.
I could feel it—the Spirit—callin' out to me.
Now I believe…and that's why
I didn't make it down to Logan tonight."[2]

When we sing this song at concerts, Steve always adds one line at the end: "Now *I* believe—and that's why she didn't make it down to Logan that night." It's his way of testifying that due to his mother's choice all those years ago, he too eventually decided to give his life to the Lord.

I want our grandchildren to know that every choice has significance, but there's one that is far more important because of its eternal impact. For that reason I pray…

For My Grandchildren

Dear Lord, I know that my grandchildren will face many choices in their lives. Of all the decisions they make, first and foremost, I pray that, like Lillian and P.J. Chapman, they'll choose to follow and serve You, the one true God. May they declare as Joshua did, "But as for me and my house, we will serve the LORD."

I pray they will choose faith—strong faith in You with no doubting. And in those times when they're tempted to waver in their resolve to trust You because they're being tossed about by the winds and waves of change, I pray they'll stand steadfast and sure in their devotion to You.

Help my grandchildren listen to godly advice and refuse to walk in the ways of fools who trust their own hearts and lean on their own understanding. Remind them to acknowledge You in all their ways and that You will make their paths straight. I thank You for guiding them so they'll make wise decisions.

Please keep my grandchildren's minds alert and fully sober so they'll set their hopes on the grace that is found in Your Son, the Lord Jesus Christ. I pray they'll choose to not conform to evil desires but, as Your children, will live holy in You.

And, Father, I want my grandchildren to make choices that will benefit the coming generations and make it easier for their grandchildren to walk in Your truth.

In Jesus' name, amen.

Joshua 24:15; James 1:6-8; Proverbs 12:15; Proverbs 3:5-6; 1 Peter 1:13-15

2

Calling God "Daddy"

I pray that my grandchildren
will always know how much
God enjoys hearing them call His name.

"Pa-ah"

We're not quite sure how it happened, but when our first grandchild got old enough to give us names, Annie became DeDe and I became PaPa. Neither of us have the slightest idea where our titles came from, but at least they're easy to say. And Annie decided that DeDe was just fine since it sounded a little younger than "Grannie Annie."

Though PaPa was easy to say, I was a little surprised when the pronunciation of it became a bit of a challenge for one of our granddaughters when she started forming words. For several weeks I was just "Pa." Then she caught on from the other grandkids that my name had two syllables. That's when I became "Pa-ah." There was such warmth and affection in the way she addressed me, and each time I heard her say it she had my complete attention.

I wondered, *Is this how our heavenly Father feels when He hears one of His children calling out His name? Is that why He listens to our prayers and grants our requests? Like I enjoy hearing "Pa-ah," surely He must love to hear His name spoken by His children when we say, "Abba...Father...Papa!"*

Eventually my granddaughter learned to say PaPa, but as long as I live I'll remember how much I liked hearing "Pa-ah." The memory will always remind me to pray that all of my grandkids understand how much God enjoys hearing the sound of their voices when they say His name.

For My Grandchildren

Heavenly Father, thank You that You've given me access to Your holy presence through the finished work of Your Son, Jesus, on the cross. I'm humbled that You allow me to come into Your presence, bringing my praises and petitions to You. Oh, how grateful I am, Abba Father, that You've granted Your children the honor of calling You "Daddy"! You are indeed the Creator of all humankind. I stand in awe of Your mighty power. You adopt into Your family only those who surrender their lives to the Lord Jesus Christ, who is our direct and only way to You. I pray each of my grandchildren will come into a relationship with You that is intimate and loving. I pray they'll always see You as their loving heavenly Daddy and know they are always welcome to come and eat at Your table.

I pray in Jesus' name, amen.

Hebrews 10:19; Ephesians 3:11-12; Galatians 3:26; Romans 8:15; Mark 14:36; Romans 9:4-8; Isaiah 40:28-31; John 14:21

3

Escaping Sin

I pray my grandchildren will be
fully committed to Jesus in a personal,
intimate relationship.

Bob and Me

It was a decision that all the family was excited about. Well, everyone but me (Annie). Past experience had taught me that what starts out as a total family commitment can quickly turn into my sole responsibility. Pushing my reservations aside, I agreed that a dog could be added to the family fold. Calls were made, and a time was set. Steve and the children would drive to the location where a fluffy puppy would become part of the Chapman lineage. They eagerly shared all the details when they returned with the new wriggly little Chapman.

There were several black-and-white canines from which to choose. As they played with one another, rolling and tumbling, they seemed unaware of the three sets of eyes glued to their every move. Then, from the back of the wire-cage kennel, one little pup locked eyes with the leader of the outside pack. Steve watched as the puppy—the one that would soon be named Bob—moved to the front of the cage. *Yes*, Steve thought, *this will be the one we'll share our lives with.*

The small dog may have thought he'd chosen his new family, but, of course, it was Steve who invited him into our world.

I identify with "Bob the dog" in a way. At one time, we were both locked in cages, unable to free ourselves. Bob's cage was made of heavy-gauge, steel wire. Mine was made out of the heaviness of sin and shame. Steve went looking for Bob and found him. God came looking for me.

Bob's part was to look to Steve; my part was to look to God. Bob found a home that lasted 12 years until he passed away. My home with the Lord will last my lifetime on earth and then for eternity.

How I long for our grandchildren to be found by God. How I long for them to look to Him for their salvation and freedom. I hope they'll spend the rest of their time on earth and then eternity with the Master of their souls. With this in mind, I pray…

For My Grandchildren

God, with a grateful heart I bring my grandchildren to Your throne of grace. Oh how merciful of You to provide salvation as a free gift and allow us to be part of Your family. Without the loving sacrifice of Jesus on the cross and His glorious resurrection from the dead, we would be without hope. I pray my grandchildren will come to know Jesus in an intimate way and grow in His likeness each day.

You've given us a commandment that we love one another, even as You loved us. I pray my grandkids will live in such a way that the world will know they are *Your* children because of the great love they have for others.

Remind my grandchildren to set their hearts on things above, where You, Lord Jesus, are seated at the right hand of the Father. I pray they will know that righteousness comes through faith in You alone. I want my grandchildren to truly know and grow more and more in love with You each day.

In Jesus' name, amen.

Hebrews 4:16; John 13:34; 1 Corinthians 9:24-25; Colossians 3:1-2; Ephesians 2:8-9; Philippians 3:7-10

4

Resting in Tranquility

I pray my grandchildren will
learn the value of resting.

At Grandma's House

My grandchildren love to hear stories about my childhood. One of the fondest memories I (Annie) have shared is about spending five glorious days each summer at my Grandma Eckard's house. The very thought of it today takes my mind back to a time when life, at least for a little while, was tranquil and, best of all, restful.

At Grandma Eckard's house I got to be the "only child" since all her children were raised. This was a special treat because at home I was the fourth of six children living with my parents in a small, four-room house. As far as I was concerned, having my own room and a bed to myself was equivalent to staying in a five-star hotel. It didn't matter that my resort retreat was an aging, two-story, clapboard house in desperate need of a fresh coat of paint.

At Grandma's house there were no chores for me to do. I didn't have to help with milking the cows, slopping the hogs, feeding the chickens, or taking care of my two younger sisters. In fact, there was nothing for me to do. It was a vacation consisting of rocking and talking on the front porch with Grandma. At her house I learned how sweet rest can be.

My two bachelor uncles who lived with Grandma made my vacation even more special. Uncle Raymond would go to town and bring back snacks and treats I never had at home: soda pop, M&M candies, doughnuts, and canned potted meat. I looked forward to those few days from one year to the next.

There were amenities lacking at Grandma's house that might have posed a problem for some children. I didn't mind that she had no electricity, no running water, no indoor plumbing, no toys, no swing sets, and, of course, no television or other modern technical trinkets that my grandchildren use for entertainment and recreation. I can't even remember having a ball to play with. All I remember is sitting on the front porch and listening as Grandma talked.

I knew how to get the conversation started. All I had to say was, "Grandma, tell me about your brothers and sisters when you were growing up." Although I'd heard most of the stories many times, I never tired of hearing them, and it seemed that she never tired of telling them. Recounting the events allowed her to revisit the people she missed and still loved dearly.

A faraway look would come to her eyes as she spoke. She would look straight ahead as though she were seeing a time that still existed— and all that was missing was her presence there. She would cry when she talked about the day her little brother Granvell asked his mom for a piece of chicken she was frying. He was told he'd have to wait until it finished cooking. Before the chicken was ready, the little boy was dead of the dreaded scarlet fever. Oh how Grandma grieved that Granvell didn't get to eat one last piece of chicken. Sad stories like these, as well as others that were more lighthearted, were told on that old front porch. For a little while I got to live those times with Grandma.

Grandma Eckard's house was only two miles from where my parents lived, but when I was there it felt like I was a million miles away. Even now I feel that faraway feeling that was due to my perspective as a child. I also realize that it was likely Grandma had things she could have…should have…been doing instead of sitting with me, but she sat with me and focused on my visit. In fact, I don't recall ever seeing my grandmother that she didn't have an apron on, so I know she constantly worked. Yet, somehow she made time to sit with me. What a great example she was as a grandmother. Even though she never met her great-great-grandchildren who now come to my house, they have her to thank each time I invite them to my back porch so we can spend time together.

Though my grandkids don't live on an extremely busy dairy farm like I did, their lives are abuzz with homeschooling, church activities, ballet, and music lessons. There are plenty of interests to steal their attention and keep them from resting. My hope is that they will learn at my house what I learned at my Grandma Eckard's house—to sit for a while and rest and listen. That's why I pray...

For My Grandchildren

Father, in these crazy days filled with actions and distractions of every kind, I pray You will help my grandchildren understand the value of rest. Even though productivity is nearly worshiped in our world today, I ask You to help them not succumb to the deceptions that they are what they do and that their value is found in what they accomplish.

Please help them understand that they were designed by You to need rest. After all, You created this magnificent universe and then rested from Your labors. There remains a rest for Your people. The ones who have entered Your rest also rest from their works as You did Yours. Help my grandchildren see the importance of stepping aside and embracing the blessing of inactivity.

Even as You, Lord Jesus, found it necessary to get away by Yourself to a place of quiet and repose, guide my grandchildren to a peaceful, alone place where they can rest from the toils and stresses of their day. Help them seek rest for their hearts and souls. May they come to You when they're weary and heavy-laden from troubles. You've promised to provide rest for their souls. I hope they'll take up Your yoke and learn from You because You are gentle and humble in heart. In You they will find rest because Your yoke is an easy one and Your burden isn't too heavy.

Please lead my grandchildren to the cool, green pastures of Your presence, where they can rest by the still waters and be restored. And it's all right with me if those still waters are found on my back porch.

In Jesus' name, amen.

Genesis 2:2; Hebrews 4:9-11; Mark 6:31; Matthew 11:28-30; Psalm 23

5

Achieving Good Health

I pray that my grandchildren
will know good health.

Healthy Bodies

When I (Steve) watch my grandchildren tumble, jump, run, climb, run some more, jump some more, do the splits, and contort their flexible bodies into shapes that defy the law of physiques, I sometimes say to myself, "I wish I could move like that." But the truth is that it wouldn't be a good idea at my age because if I made even one of their moves (intentional or not), something might pop or break.

Because I've entered my "brittle years," when parts of me are hurting that never hurt before, I've seriously considered writing a revised version of an old familiar song:

> The ankle brace connected to the knee brace
> The knee brace connected to the hip brace
> The hip brace connected to the back brace
> O hear the hurt, I'm so sore...

For now I'll remain grateful for the pains I don't have and enjoy watching my rambunctious grandchildren display their youthful vigor.

The wellness of our grandkids is a constant concern for their parents, and it is extremely important to grandparents as well. Because it is, Annie and I do what we can to contribute to our grandchildren's good health. For example, when they're with us, we're careful to steer them away from food and drink that is nutritionally worthless. Except for the ice-cream treats we keep in the freezer (next to the frozen pizza), they mostly get fruits, veggies, whole-grain cereal (the kind that does not have the colors of the rainbow and is not full of sugar), and other whole foods.

Also, while they're at our house, we monitor their whereabouts to make sure they keep a safe distance from the highway we live beside. We make sure our knives and other potentially harmful household items, including firearms, medicines, cleansers, and matches, are out of reach. And we're attentive so they avoid overly risky activities, such as climbing too high in our backyard trees.

Even with all of our watchfulness and the good care they get from their parents, we're aware that the good health of our grandkids is a fragile thing. Accidents happen, and life-altering sicknesses are possible. With this reality in mind, I'm compelled to pray...

For My Grandchildren

O Lord, You are the Maker of my grandchildren, and You do all things well. Their frames weren't hidden from Your view when they were formed in the secret place. You wove together all their parts. Your eyes saw what was happening, and You knew that what You did was good. Then You took out Your book and wrote down all their days. Yes, even before there was one day lived, You knew what was going to happen. You are awesome, God.

I understand that the main benefit of having good health is that it allows us to use these bodies to serve You. I pray that my grandchildren will embrace this truth, and that whatever they do in word or deed they'll do it to Your glory, giving thanks to You, their Creator, all the days of their lives.

Help my grandchildren regard their bodies as temples—sanctuaries—where You reside. Remind them daily that their bodies aren't their own. They've been bought with a price; therefore, they are to honor You with their whole bodies.

O Father, in those times when my grandchildren's health is threatened, and they face possible injury or disease, remind them that they can call on You as their Healer…that through the sacrifice of Jesus, Your Son, their health may be restored.

Show my grandchildren the importance of feeding their bodies healthy, nutritious foods; the value of getting plenty of strength-building exercise; and the vital concept that they need to allow their bodies time to repair by getting enough sleep. And, of utmost importance, help them keep their bodies free from sinful behaviors that could threaten their physical and mental health and, in turn, might harm them spiritually and emotionally.

I pray all this in the mighty name of Jesus, amen.

Psalm 139:14-16; Colossians 3:17; 1 Corinthians 6:19-20;
Isaiah 53:6

6

Knowing God's Word

I pray that my grandchildren will
know, love, and obey God's Word.

Nine Mile Creek

I (Annie) was raised along a narrow, winding tributary of the
Kanawha River in Mason County, West Virginia. The shallow body
of water was named for the distance our small community was from
the county seat. Nine Mile Creek was our primary source of recreation
as kids. When our work was done and Mom couldn't stand to have us
underfoot any longer, she'd send us out the door. We'd go down to the
creek to play.

We had a lot of fun skipping rocks across the surface, catching craw-
dads using an old, rusty coffee can, jumping in the water and playing,
and seeing who could hold their breath the longest under the murky
water. We'd stay until our mom called us back to the house or we had
to do evening chores.

It wasn't until I left home years later that I realized some of the
neighbors up the road were using our little water wonderland as a part
of their septic system. In other words, they daily dumped their raw sew-
age into the creek. We thought our playground was made up of just
fun, muddy clay and our swimming hole was simply a little cloudy. We
didn't understand that it was something far different—actually dan-
gerously different.

Today, so many children are playing in the "creek of this world,"
and their parents seem unaware of the many hidden dangers lurking in
the depths. When I see, for example, what's presented as family friendly

programming on television, when I look at the clothes designed for our grandkids to wear, when I listen to what is offered on the radio, when I see the trailers for the new movies, and when I hear the news from around the corner and around the world, my mind goes back to the situation at Nine Mile Creek. My grandchildren live in a world that is diseased and littered with the refuse of sinful filth. For them to survive and thrive and, hopefully, make a difference in the world, they have to know the Truth with a capital "T." That Truth is found in God's written Word.

If our grandchildren aren't taught to love and to know and to obey the clear truths in God's Word, they could end up swimming in the contaminated waters of the lies and deceptions that flow through this present age. In a time when wrong is often declared right, they need the clarity of God's Word to help them recognize the causes for the cloudiness in the stream they're playing in. I want them to avoid being spiritually sickened. This is why I often pray…

For My Grandchildren

Dear Lord, thank You for providing Your written Word that flows as the only perfectly clean source of truth. I pray my grandchildren will immerse themselves in it, enjoy it, and drink of it daily so they'll know how to live pure before You. All Scripture is "God-breathed" and profitable for teaching, reproof, correction, and training in right living. I'm so grateful that because of Your Word, my grandchildren can be competent and equipped for every good work.

I hope Your holy Scriptures will be the place they go to find hope. As they meditate on it day and night, may they be careful to do according to all that is written in it, for then You will make their ways prosper, and they will have success.

Help my grandchildren know that Your Word is living and active, sharper than any two-edged sword, piercing to the division of soul and spirit, of joints and of marrow, and discerning the very thoughts and intentions of their hearts. Sanctify them in the truth—Your Word.

Encourage my grandchildren to store Your Word in their hearts so they won't sin against You. Guide them to seek You and not wander away from the truths found in the holy Scriptures. This world has grass that will wither and flowers that will fade, but Your Word, O Lord, will stand forever. Reveal to my grandchildren that Your Word is not only a source of life but also a lamp to their feet and a light to their path. I long for them to walk on the narrow way that leads to Your marvelous presence.

I pray this in Jesus' name, amen.

2 Timothy 3:16-17; Joshua 1:8; Hebrews 4:12-13; Psalm 1:2; John 17:17; Psalm 119:9-11; Isaiah 40:8; Psalm 119:105

7

Feeling Safe and Secure

I pray that my grandchildren
will always know the joy of
being in a family who loves them
and has their backs.

A Safe Place

Johnny slowly dragged himself through the front door of his house. Eighth grade was not supposed to be so hard. Being the target of the class bully had changed Johnny's school experience from being a place of learning to a dreaded torture chamber.

After being harassed and tormented all day long, he came into the house with his shoulders drooping and his eyes red from tears of frustration and degradation. Keeping the abuse a secret hadn't helped the situation. He knew it was time to come clean and tell his folks what he was up against. For far too long he'd denied the truth. Now it was time to admit that he couldn't handle the bullying alone. He needed his parents' help.

How relieved he was that confiding to his folks wasn't as hard to do as he'd anticipated. His dad didn't belittle him for crying about his hurt feelings. His mother, as he'd suspected, was furious—but not with him. Her ire was directed to the brute that was using her son as a verbal punching bag.

After allowing Johnny time to unburden his heart, a course of action was put into place. As their conversation wound down, Johnny looked at his mom, his dad, and his two siblings who had joined them in the family meeting. Then he said something that turned a serious discussion into a hug fest. He said, "No matter how bad it gets at school, I know when I come through the front door of our house that I'm in a safe place."

Safe. That's what home is supposed to be. A haven. A secure place to land. A soft shoulder to lean on. A harbor from the storms of life. I want my grandchildren to always feel the kind of closeness to their families that Johnny felt to his. I want my grandchildren to know they can always count on their extended family to back them up. That's why I pray…

For My Grandchildren

God, I know You've blessed me with our children and now with our grandchildren. They are indeed a heritage from You and a wonderful gift from Your hand. As blessed as I am to have them, I pray they will feel equally blessed to be part of Your extended family. You've promised that if they're taught Your ways and choose to follow You, You'll grant them peace and righteousness. You'll be established in their lives. I earnestly ask that You keep tyranny far from them so they'll have nothing to fear.

As their grandparent, help me be an encouragement to them. Show me how to let them know I too am here for them. As they are instructed in the way they should go, give me the insights I need to reinforce the truths presented to them. May my grandchildren know that their family stands beside them to help bear their burdens, to forgive their failings, and to provide a safe place for them to live. Give my extended family and me compassionate actions we can do that will help my grandchildren…

- learn what real love is
- find kindness not criticism
- hear cheers not jeers

- experience generosity, not jealousy
- find support, but not enabling
- find an advocate, not an adversary
- find mercy, not judgment
- feel challenged, not crushed

In Jesus' name I ask these things for my grandchildren, amen.

Psalm 127:3-5; Colossians 3:12-13; Isaiah 54:13-14; Proverbs 1:8-9; 1 Corinthians 13:4-7

8

Honoring Their Parents

I pray that my grandchildren
will honor their father and mother.

Helping the Grands Bless Their Parents

The challenge of raising our two children yielded a saying that Annie now offers mothers as both a fair warning and an encouragement. It's based on Proverbs 31:28: "Right now they rise up and say, 'Fix me some breakfast!,' but someday they'll rise up and call you 'blessed.'"

Annie knows, of course, that the words "rise up and call [you] blessed" are not referring to a time of day, but to a time in life. It's not reasonable to expect average kids to wake up each day thinking of something to say to encourage the adults in their lives. Instead, their first thoughts are about *their* bladders, *their* appetites, *their* thirsts, *their* toys, *their* entertainment, and every other *their*—except for the ones that would make Mom and Dad and grandparents feel honored.

One thing Annie and I can do until our grandchildren outgrow their "me" years is encourage them to honor their parents. We can do this in some nonverbal ways too. For instance, we can remind them that they can bless their mom and dad by being obedient, helping with the cleaning around the house and yard, being courteous to visitors, and not being selfish with their possessions. We can even show them how to make their parents gifts using various art supplies. As motivation, we can also show them how Jesus brought glory to His heavenly Father by completing the tasks He was given (John 17:4).

The good news *we* can offer their parents is that time and maturity will pull back the selfishness blinders from most children's eyes so they can see what their parents actually do for them. When that "eureka moment" happens and their children's thankful feelings are put into words, these parents will be shocked and amazed and pleased. I'll never forget seeing one mother's reaction when she was honored before a live audience on national television.

On the show *American Idol*, a young singer named Lauren Alaina was one of two finalists. During the heavily viewed closing segment, she sang a song called "Like My Mother Does" that she dedicated to her mother. The cameras occasionally focused on Lauren's mom sitting in the audience with tears of joy streaming down her face.

What the nation didn't know was that in the den of our house I got to see the surprise and delight on another mother's face when it was announced which song Lauren was going to sing. Annie sat straight up in her chair and shot a glance at me. "Did you know this was going to happen?" I answered, "Yes, I did! And, baby, you deserve for the world to hear this song." You see, that song was inspired by Annie. Our son, Nathan, had come to recognize the greatness of his mother's investment in his life. Intending to honor her, he took his idea to his fellow songwriters, Liz Rose and Nikki Williams, and they all worked to put his words of thanks to music. I was privileged to watch Proverbs 31:28 take place in real life, in real time. (You can watch Lauren Alaina's performance of "Like My Mother Does" on YouTube.)

One other song that was written to bless a mom and dad came from the heart of a fellow Tennessean who contacted me via email and asked for my help with his lyrics. His parents were entering their nineties, and he wanted to honor them at their church. Here is the blessing Danny bestowed on his parents.

Hey, Mom & Dad

Hey, Mom and Dad, I'm so glad you stayed around to see
Your three boys grow into men you believed that we could be.
You loved us and you kept us, taught us how to do our best,
And you forgave us when we put your sweet love to the test.

I just want to let you know how much I love you.
It seems so right to say it in this song
'Cause you've been the melody that goes with all the memories.
It makes my heart want to sing along.
I thank God I grew up in your home.

Hey, Mom and Dad, I'm so glad you're here to hear the sound
Of laughter of a grandchild—it's where your love is found.
And as you go, I hope you know we'll all be right behind,
Walking in the truth you gave us in your light that always
    shines.

I could never buy your kind of love—the price would be too
    great.
How blessed we are that you chose to give it all away.[3]

Whether it's done with lyrics and music, prose to read, a painting
for a refrigerator, a hug, a smile, a clean room or completed task, I'm
hopeful that our grandchildren will find ways to bless their fathers and
mothers. I know that, ultimately, God too will be honored. For that
reason I pray...

For My Grandchildren

Dear God, You've lavished Your fatherly love on me, and for that I say a sincere thanks. You said that when I honor my earthly father and mother my days will be prolonged in the land You've given me. I desire this reward for my grandchildren. Please open their eyes to see how their good behavior and kind actions toward their parents can bless them. Help me assist them with following the command to honor their folks by encouraging them to say words that are sweet like Yours, by being obedient, considerate, courteous, loving, and thankful. May their days be long on the earth as a result, and may the hearts of their parents be filled with the joy of their children's blessing.

In Christ's name, amen.

Exodus 20:12; Ephesians 6:1; Psalm 119:103; 1 Peter 3:8;
Titus 3:2; Romans 12:10

9

Overcoming Obstacles

I pray that my grandchildren
will not allow something they can change
to limit their lives.

The Cardboard Steinway

Steve and I have a piano in our home, and our granddaughters enjoy pecking around on it. One day while they were visiting, I sat down and played one of my favorite old gospel songs. One of our granddaughters came into the living room with a totally puzzled look on her face. She stared at me as she stood by the piano. I stopped playing and asked why she looked so bewildered.

"I had no idea you could play the piano," she replied. "When did you learn to do it?"

I knew she wanted to learn to play, and I thought she might enjoy hearing how I'd developed an interest. I told her this story:

> Growing up I wanted more than anything to learn to play the piano. Being from a large family who lived in a very small house, and not having the extra money to spend on a piano, becoming a skilled pianist was not going to be part of my future.
>
> However, my desire to learn to masterfully tickle the ivories overrode any obstacles that stood in my way. And believe me, there were some obstacles. The first one was a big one. We didn't have a piano. Second, if we'd owned a piano, we didn't have any money to pay a teacher. Third, as far as I

knew, no one in our small community taught piano. No instrument. No money. No instructor. What was I going to do?

They say necessity is the mother of invention, and I believe whoever "they" are hit the nail right on the head. I found a long, rectangular piece of heavy cardboard and a black Magic Marker. I headed to our local church. At that time people didn't lock the church doors so folks could come and go as they wanted or needed. I went in and walked to the front of the sanctuary where the piano was.

Sitting on the stool of the old upright, I counted the keys and then drew the keyboard on the piece of cardboard. Knowing where middle C was located, I figured out an old familiar hymn and memorized the sound of each key. Then I took my cardboard piano home and practiced diligently. When I could, I would go back to the church to try out my skills on an actual piano—seeing if my fingers were placed correctly and if it sounded right.

Now, all these years later, I still enjoy playing the spinet piano we purchased. I wouldn't say I play skillfully, but I play well enough to enjoy an old hymn now and then.

Although my cardboard piano was thrown into the garbage heap long ago, my joy remains that I refused to allow obstacles to keep me from achieving my goal. But every time I play my piano, I can see that "cardboard Steinway" in my mind.

The look on my granddaughter's face told me she enjoyed the story. One of my main reasons for telling it was to plant a seed in her heart that she should never allow something she can change to limit her life. Until she fully understands and embraces this attitude, I will pray…

For My Grandchildren

Dear Father, I know my grandchildren will encounter many stumbling blocks on their roads of life. Please help them see that these obstacles aren't meant to stop their forward progress; instead, they are mere stepping-stones that can help them reach even higher and achieve even more. You promised that my grandchildren can do all things through Christ if they call on His strength. With humans, things are impossible, but with Your help nothing is impossible. Encourage them, Father. Give them creative ideas of how to accomplish the goals You've put in their hearts. Enlarge the places of their tents; stretch the curtains wide to make room for all You want to do in their lives. Don't let them quit; remind them that You are the help they need.

When they're having a hard time getting through school, experiencing what feels like insurmountable challenges with a job, or suffering from exhaustion from raising their children, remind them they are not in the fight alone. You are with them. Give them courage to press through and never give up. Their lives don't need to be limited just because life is hard.

With You as their hope and their help, I know they'll thrive. I ask that You give them a clear vision of *what* and *who* You intend them to be and become. I pray they will accept the unchangeable but change the unacceptable. I know You'll lead them to overcome and be victorious.

May this prayer be answered because I ask in Jesus' name, amen.

Philippians 4:12-13; Matthew 19:26; Isaiah 54:2; Genesis 18:14; Isaiah 59:1; Jeremiah 32:17; Luke 1:37

10

Enjoying Laughter

I pray that my grandchildren will always
know the medicinal value of humor.

"Humories"

One thing Annie and I have discovered about grandchildren is that
as long as there are youngsters around, there'll be no shortage of things
to laugh about. Let me share two of my favorite "humories" (a word
Annie and I made up for the laugh memories they provide).

- One of our grandkids tore the last page out of the popular children's book *The Little Engine That Could.* When
  their dad discovered there was a missing page, he suspected
  whose handiwork it was and asked, "Did you rip this
  page out of this book?" The child sheepishly smiled and
  answered, "I think I did, I think I did, I think I did…"

- Another grandchild overheard her mom talking to a
  friend at church. Their conversation was about a lady in
  the congregation who was experiencing some health concerns regarding her heart. One comment said during their
  exchange was "I heard she has heart trouble in her genes."
  After church was over and the granddaughter was headed
  to the car with her family, she asked her mom, "Why
  would your friend have heart trouble in her pants?"

What's especially interesting about all the humories we've collected
through the years is that the young grandkids rarely know they're

creating them. However, we've noticed as they get older they start to catch on to the fact that their antics make us laugh, and they enjoy it. And that's exactly what we hope for—that they will understand how much more enjoyable life can be when good, clean fun that creates laughter is cultivated in a family. For that reason, I pray…

For My Grandchildren

Dear Lord, I'm very aware that a joyful heart is the medicine that can heal a crushed spirit that has dried up the bones. Thank You for Your promise to fill our mouths with laughter and our lips with shouts of joy. Part of Your plan is for us to have times to laugh and dance, along with times of weeping. May my grandchildren know a good balance between the two. I hope their faces will often reflect the cheer that You supply abundantly.

Help them create godly boundaries so the humor they prefer will not be founded in ungodliness or foolishness or be brought on by alcohol or drugs. Instead, may they enjoy comedy that contributes to fun and thanksgiving.

Most of all, Father, let their gladness ultimately be found in You. Because of Your righteousness imparted to them, they always will have cause to shout for joy.

In Jesus' sweet name, amen.

Proverbs 17:22; Job 8:21; Ecclesiastes 3:4; Ephesians 5:4; Psalm 32:11

11

Receiving God's Grace

I pray my grandchildren will
not let the past determine their futures.

Rahab the Redeemed

Of all the characters whose failures and sins are laid bare for my
grandchildren to see in the Bible, one of my favorites is Rahab (Joshua
2). Day after day Rahab practiced her trade that involved continu-
ous acts of harlotry and immorality. I (Annie) am sure she could have
found a different source of means or turned to her family for support,
but she chose to sell her body.

Some biblical scholars have tried to "clean up" the account of
Rahab by denying she was a prostitute. Some refer to her as an "inn-
keeper," a landlady who housed merchants in town on business. But
the Scriptures don't portray her that way. Not only is she identified as
a harlot in the Old Testament, but Paul and James also refer to her as a
harlot in the New Testament (Joshua 2:1; Hebrews 11:31; James 2:25).

I believe God wanted us to know the truth about Rahab so we
would understand His heart a little better. There is great comfort in
knowing that God is more concerned with our futures than He is with
our pasts. Oh, how grateful we all should be to know that He looks
at the truth and not just the facts. He offers us His grace (unmerited
favor) through His Son, Jesus Christ, as the only means to salvation,
to being united with Him. Our efforts to be "good enough" aren't sufficient. And that's why I love the story of Rahab.

Even though she lived the life of a prostitute, she didn't die as one.

After helping to rescue and hide the spies Joshua sent into Jericho, Rahab's life was transformed. The gratitude of one of the spies named Salmon changed from appreciation to affection. He married her, and she lived out her days among the people of God. Not only was her life changed, but her family tree took a dramatic turn. She became the great-great-grandmother of King David—and that placed her in the lineage of our Lord and Savior, Jesus Christ!

Although Rahab made some really bad choices, the last chapter of her life had a happy ending. Yes, the facts of her past were ugly, but the truth was gloriously beautiful. She turned her faith from pagan gods to fully embracing faith in her heavenly Father. She was indeed a prostitute, and even today when her name is mentioned the title "harlot" is usually attached. That might be a fact, but the truth is that in heaven she's known as "Rahab the Redeemed."

I want my grandchildren to know that if they make mistakes, if they choose a sinful path, failure doesn't have to be final. Our God is the God of second, third, and even more chances. That's why I pray...

For My Grandchildren

Dear heavenly Father, help my grandchildren not let past sin or failure define their futures. Thank You for the examples of those who have gone before us that show Your great kindness, Your compassion for sinners, and Your willingness to forgive and redeem. I pray my grandchildren won't dwell on the past, whether the former things were victories or failures. You've told us that You're doing a new thing. You've promised to make a way in the desert and streams in the wasteland. You're a good hiding place in bad times. You welcome anyone looking for help. God, You are merciful and loving. For that I give You praise.

No matter what has happened in the past or what challenges they face today or tomorrow, remind my grandchildren that there is always hope in You. Your steadfast love never ceases.

Your mercies never come to an end—they are new every morning. Great is Your faithfulness!

I want my grandchildren to know Your promises are true, and that You will never leave them nor forsake them. You're patient with them with the hope that they'll come to You. Give my grandchildren peace and protection so they'll not be afraid or suffer shame. Let them know they need not fear disgrace because You do not humiliate Your children. Your grace is so great they can forget the shame of their youth and remember no more the reproach of their loss. For You, Lord, are their Maker. The LORD Almighty is Your name.

In Jesus' name, amen.

Isaiah 43:18-21; 2 Corinthians 5:17; Nahum 1:7; Lamentations 3:21-23; Hebrews 13:5; 2 Peter 3:9; Isaiah 54:4-5; Philippians 3:13-14

12

Understanding Forgiveness

*I pray my grandchildren will
know the importance and benefits
of forgiving offenses.*

The Sure Cure for Burns

As much as I (Steve) would like to assume that my grandchildren would never feel the heartbreak of betrayal, the pain of rejection, the wounds of abuse, or the sting of insult, my life experiences, as well as the Word of God, have taught me they will. Luke 17:1 says that offenses come to us all, which means it's impossible to avoid them. Since we have no option but to deal with the inevitability of these transgressions, our only hope for successfully doing so lies in *how* we respond.

To help my grandkids, I want to teach them to recognize that while all types of assaults will hurt and must be eventually forgiven, it's incorrect to assume that all are equal. Offenses to the heart are similar to burns on the body. While all burns are painful, they can range in severity from the discomfort of a sunburn to the life-threatening agony of an electrical burn that can damage internal organs.

Most sunburns are easy to remedy by getting out of the burning rays, applying a cool cloth to the scorched flesh, and administering some kind of over-the-counter ointment. However, a severe electrical burn has to be treated with urgency and extensive care. The possibility of the person going into shock, contracting infection, and facing possible surgery or even death makes this type of burn extremely serious. Professional intervention is not only smart, it's imperative.

When it comes to personal offenses, some are like a sunburn. There are things that happen that might be upsetting, but given some time and a little attention we heal and then forgive. Most of the time we even forget what seemed so terrible. But like the electrical-burn victim who suffers long-term damage and needs professional assistance to heal, there are some offenses that are very difficult to heal from, forgive, and, more than likely, can't be forgotten. Abandonment, abuses of all kinds, rejection, and betrayals are a few of the wrongs that can scar a person to the very core of his or her being. Then the person may feel damaged beyond repair. For those who have been hurt so deeply, it's even more important for them to heal, forgive, and then let go of the offense because if they don't, it will continue to burn and do even greater damage.

As my grandchildren progress through time, I know they'll encounter offenses that will range from playmates taking toys from them to boyfriends/girlfriends breaking their hearts. From experience I can tell them that in order for the "burn" to heal, they'll need to *forgive* like they want to be forgiven.

When the disciples asked Jesus to teach them to pray, He taught them what we now call the Lord's Prayer. There's a statement in that prayer that catches my heart every time I pray it: "Forgive us our debts, as we also have forgiven our debtors" (Matthew 6:12). Does that mean if we don't forgive others, God will not forgive us? There are many interpretations of what is meant by Jesus' statement, but one thing I've concluded is that if my heart is full of unforgiveness, there'll be no room to receive forgiveness. Because of this, forgiving is one of the critical skills my grandchildren need to develop.

They also need to know that people aren't designed to carry bitterness. Holding on to it can take a toll on their bodies in the forms of heart disease, strokes, depression, elevated blood pressure, mental disorders, cancer, and many digestive problems.

Though it's impossible to avoid offenses, God has made it possible for us to forgive them, but we need His help to do it. I hope my grandchildren will call on Him for that needed help. That's why I pray...

For My Grandchildren

Dear Father, of all the burning wounds the enemy of our souls attempts to inflict on us, unforgiveness can be the most damaging because it severely distracts us from receiving Your love. I pray that my grandchildren will find strength in You to forgive others, just as in Christ You forgive them. I hope they'll forgive with hearts that know the blessed relief of being forgiven by You and by the people around them.

Thank You, Father, that You don't treat my grandchildren as their sins deserve or repay them according to their iniquities. As high as the heavens are above the earth, so great is Your love for Your children. As far as the east is from the west, You've removed their transgressions from them. You know how my grandchildren are formed. You remember that they are dust, yet Your compassion covers them.

How gracious You are to not remember or keep a record of their sins. Help my grandchildren to do the same. Remind them that through Your love and power working in their lives, they can forgive those who hurt them.

In Jesus' name, amen.

Ephesians 4:32; Matthew 6:15; Psalm 103:10-12; Psalm 130:3-4; Hebrews 10:15-17

13

Choosing Courage

*I pray that my grandchildren will
choose courage over fear.*

The 500-Foot Drop

Our friend Ilene Wilson gave two of our granddaughters the opportunity to ride her horses. They fell in love with all things equestrian that day. I (Steve) warned my son-in-law that their ride may eventually cost him some cash if he bends to their newly found desire to have a horse. The experience also gave me a chance to tell the girls about a scary moment I had with a horse while elk hunting in Montana.

My ride into a remote region of the Gallatin National Forest was on the back of a coal-black, sure-footed, strong, and very tall horse that my hunting guide had provided. As the critter carried me higher and higher up the mountainside, I noticed that the trail kept getting narrower. Eventually we came to an area where there was a rock wall on my right that my leg scraped due to the width of the trail. That wasn't so bad...and everything was fine until we rounded a bend. What I saw on my left was a sight that caused me to shiver in fear. I was looking at a drop of 500 feet or so.

There was no guardrail to give me comfort as the horse slowly sauntered along. I held my breath as I sat in the saddle and silently prayed against everything from mountain lions that could spook the horse and cause it to bolt to an earthquake that might shake the trail beneath the horse's shoes. I couldn't dismount because there wasn't room. All I could do was grip the saddle horn with both hands and squeeze the horse's girth with my trembling legs.

With about another 50 yards to go before we passed what I now refer to as the "Have Mercy" section of the trail, I was compelled to find courage somewhere. Finally it dawned on me that my horse wanted to get back home too. In fact, he seemed very calm and confident. I also noticed his head never turned like mine did to look at the dangerous drop. He was focused on the trail ahead.

Drawing on the animal's confidence he seemed to have about treading the trail, I realized my fear was subsiding. Basically I didn't just borrow courage from the horse; I took it, and it became my own. By the time we were at the end of the perilous section, I was smiling. My restored confidence felt good.

I offered this story to help my grandchildren understand what it means in the Bible when we're instructed to "take courage" (Matthew 14:27; Acts 23:11). There has to be a reliable source from which to take it. That source is God, who is completely fearless. To lay claim to His provision of courage is to fully trust that He's focused on the trail and not on the deadly cliffs that line our journey through the mountains of life. I know it's not *if* my grandkids will encounter fear, but rather *when* it will happen. For this reason I pray…

For My Grandchildren

Father, the path through the world is getting more and more frightening with each passing day. Without complete assurance that You're in control of every situation, there's no way my grandkids can face these times without succumbing to fear. Knowing I can trust You in everything, I confidently bring my grandchildren to You, asking You to watch over them and teach them to "take courage." They need to know that although You command them to not be afraid, You've also promised to strengthen them, help them, and uphold them with Your righteous right hand.

Please guide my grandchildren so they'll put their faith and trust in You. You won't let them be put to shame. The strength and courage You supply will be all they need. There is no cause to tremble because You are always with them. You will never fail or forsake them.

Help my grandchildren understand that in Jesus they can have peace. In this world they'll face tribulation, but they can take courage because He has overcome the world. When my grandchildren are afraid, encourage them to put their trust in You, Father.

I know You've not given my grandchildren a spirit of timidity but of power and love and discipline. What a comfort to know that You will never leave or forsake them! I want my grandchildren to know beyond a shadow of doubt that You are their helper and that Your perfect love drives out all fear. Make this truth be a daily experience for them.

In Your Son's precious name, amen.

Isaiah 41:10; Isaiah 54:4; Deuteronomy 31:6; John 16:33;
Psalm 56:3-4; 2 Timothy 1:7; Hebrews 13:5-6; 1 John 4:18

14

Letting God Be in Control

I pray that my grandchildren will
know these three important truths:
God loves them, He's in control, and He's trustworthy.

The Big Three

I (Annie) had lunch with a longtime friend who is also a grandmother. We were catching up on all that had happened in the six-month interval since we'd last visited. I detected she had something troubling on her mind, so I asked her what was going on.

"My husband was let go of his job. Because of the bad economic situation, they just don't have the work to keep him on. We thought that was bad enough…and then he started looking for another job. Seems like he's too old and too qualified for positions that pay anywhere near what we need. At this stage in our lives, we're supposed to be getting our financial house in order so we can retire someday. At this rate, I'm going to be working into my eighties. I'm working myself to death to keep us afloat, and I'm tired. I can't quit, but I sure want to."

As my friend unloaded her burdened heart, my mind raced to the only place I could go to find help for her—the Word of God. I dug through my purse and found the piece of paper on which I'd written this encouragement:

The longer I live the less I know.
But what I know, I know for sure:

- God loves me.

- God is in control.

- I can trust Him.

My friend wrote them down on the back of a receipt and put it into her purse. I shoved my paper into the front pocket of my jeans. We left the subject of unemployment and started talking about our favorite and happier topic—our grandchildren.

A week or so later I went to a scheduled doctor's appointment. After the examination and some additional tests, he invited me into his office to talk about what he'd found. The doctor was concerned about something on the ultrasound. He talked about surgery and even used the big "C" word (cancer) as a possibility of what could be wrong. He left me alone in the room so he could confer with another physician about his findings.

As I sat there worried about what was going to happen, I slipped my hand into the front pocket of my jeans. The note was still there. I pulled it out and read the words I'd used to comfort my friend the week before. "God loves me. God is in control. I can trust Him." In that scary moment sitting in the doctor's office, those three truths were like a healing balm to my troubled soul. God used the comfort I offered to a dear friend to comfort me in my time of distress. That simple message scribbled on a small piece of paper reminded me of an enormously important truth: No matter how trying the situation may be, I don't face it alone.

A week before my scheduled surgery, I insisted that my doctor rerun the ultrasound to see if anything had changed. He warned me that the problem I had wouldn't go away on its own, but I wasn't counting on it going away on its own. I'd put my trust in a healing Jesus who can make all things right. To appease me, the doctor ordered the new test. To his surprise and my delight, there was no sign of any problem! It had disappeared! I didn't have to undergo surgery. As for my friend's husband and his job search, it ended with a position that he loves…and that pays well. To God be the glory!

Even if things had turned out differently for my friend and me, I would've done what I encourage my grandkids to do. I would have held on to the "big three" with confidence and hope. "God loves me. He's in control. I can trust Him." To do so is to stand on solid ground. I long for my grandchildren to know the comfort of these truths, so I pray…

For My Grandchildren

Dear Lord, thank You that Your grace is sufficient and You're my help in times of trouble. Reveal to my grandchildren that You love them with an everlasting love. No matter what they might face in this life, let them know they will be more than conquerors through You, the omnipotent One who loves them. May they be convinced in their hearts that neither death nor life, nor angels nor rulers, nor things present nor things to come can separate them from Your love, which is found in Christ Jesus.

Father, You are so rich in mercy. Because of Your great love, even when my grandchildren were dead in their trespasses You made a way for them to be alive in Christ. By Your grace, they will be saved!

Watch over my grandchildren and let nothing touch their lives that doesn't come through the filter of Your loving hands. You are in control, so they need not fear. Help them to always remember that all things will work together for their good because You love them and they are called according to Your purpose.

Assure my grandchildren that from the rising of the sun to the setting of the sun there is no one or no thing that can overcome or be above You. You are Lord of all! You formed light and created darkness. You create well-being; You allow calamity. Remind my grandchildren daily that many are the plans of humans, but Your purpose is what will stand. May they find comfort in knowing that Your thoughts and Your ways are higher than theirs. Show them that You allow difficult things in their lives for a purpose. You're teaching them that You are all-powerful and in control. Father, may Your name be proclaimed in all the earth.

Give my grandchildren understanding so they'll know You love them and You hold all power. Let them know they can put their full trust in You and rest in the knowledge that You love them. Help them not be afraid because You're with them always. They need not be dismayed because You are their God. If they trust You, You will strengthen them, and help them, and uphold them with Your righteous right hand.

In Jesus' name, amen.

2 Corinthians 12:9; Psalm 46:1; Romans 8:37-39; Ephesians 2:4-5; Romans 8:28; Isaiah 45:6-7; Genesis 1:3-5; Proverbs 19:21; Isaiah 55:8-11; Exodus 9:16; 1 John 4:9-10; Ephesians 3:17-19; Isaiah 41:10

15

Finding Good Friends

I pray my grandchildren will
keep good friends and be good friends.

Mom's Apple Wisdom

"If you want to know what kind of person you'll be in the future, take a look at the friends you're keeping now. If you don't believe me, watch this." These were the words of my mother on the day she instructed my sister and me (Steve) to join her in the kitchen. On the counter sat a bowl of beautiful, red, crisp apples. One by one she removed the good apples. Then she took a very rotten apple and placed it in the center at the bottom of the bowl. As she put the fresh, crisp apples back in the bowl on top of the rotten one, she said, "We'll take a look at the results in a few days."

Nearly a week later Mom brought the bowl of apples back to the table. Before she removed the apples that were on top of the bad apple, the putrid smell of rotting fruit filled the kitchen. Each good apple that touched the bad one was half-rotted away.

"Kids," she said with motherly sternness, "the Bible says, 'bad company corrupts good morals.' Don't forget it, and be careful who you associate with."

Mom didn't need to say anything else. Her life-changing point was made, and my sister and I have never forgotten it. It's a truth that I want my grandchildren to learn and embrace. The following lyric was written to help them further understand this timeless wisdom.

The Friends You Keep

William was a good boy, as good as they come.
No trouble to his mother; to his father, a good son.
But then he started running with a boy down the road.
They knew he was a bad seed when the fruit began to grow.

The friends you keep and hang around,
They can lift you up, they can take you down.
They can help you sow, but you'll be the one to reap.
You better beware of the friends you keep.

Late one summer night, he slipped out of his room,
And made his way into the town by the shadows of the moon.
There he met his new friend behind the old Dime Store.
The broken glass and the innocence lay shattered on the floor.

They took the things they wanted, and they were just about to
     go,
That's when they saw the blue lights, but William didn't know
That his friend had a thirty-eight, and when the smoke had
     cleared
The cigarettes and pocketknives would cost him twenty years.

The friends you keep and hang around,
They can lift you up, they can take you down.
They can help you sow, but you'll be the one to reap.
You better beware of the friends you keep.[4]

And that's why I continue to pray…

For My Grandchildren

Dear Lord, when I think about having and being a good friend,
my mind goes back to the friendship between David and Jonathan mentioned in the Bible. What a beautiful story of sacrifice

54

and loyalty. Your servant Jonathan endured the disapproval of his father, King Saul, and forfeited his perceived right to be the next king. Jonathan even risked his life to save David's life. After Jonathan was killed, King David showed his loyalty by caring for Jonathan's crippled son.

Lord, You command us to love each other, even as You love us. In fact, there is no love greater than this: for a friend to lay down his or her life for a friend. You've shown me that friendship is an important part of my life because it influences how I spend my time, where I choose to go, and what I choose to do. I earnestly pray for my grandchildren that they will use great wisdom in choosing their friends and exercise great loyalty in being godly friends.

Please protect my grandchildren from being deceived by the corrupted characters of those who want to lead them astray and tear them down instead of build them up. Keep bad people far from them, and grant them wisdom in choosing wisely those they call friends. You say in Your holy Word that if anyone asks for wisdom You will give it with great liberality. Encourage them to seek Your counsel when it comes to selecting the people they hang out with.

Lord, a true friend loves at all times. Give my grandchildren the joy of having and being such a friend.

In Jesus' name, amen.

1 Samuel 18–20; 2 Samuel 9; John 15:12-13; 1 Corinthians 15:33; Proverbs 17:17; James 1:5

16

Sowing for a Good Harvest

I pray that my grandchildren will
understand the laws of sowing and reaping.

The Backyard Flower Garden

It wasn't until after my mother died that I (Annie) became interested in gardening. Until then I was too busy with raising and home-schooling our children, as well as traveling with Steve as a professional musician. I didn't have time to cultivate and nurture plants. But something happened inside me after my children were grown…and especially after my mom's passing.

Even though my mother had been fully occupied with raising her brood of six and helping keep our dairy farm running with Dad, she always found time to cultivate a large vegetable garden that would help feed our family. She also surrounded herself with pots of beautiful, well-cared-for flowers. So, in honor of my mother, I decided to tackle the task of turning the two-acre lot that surrounded our home into a flower wonderland. For several years, I spent many hours a day during the garden-growing season working the land. I really enjoyed the visual bounty it brought forth.

After our first grandchild came along, my attention was once again diverted from growing begonias and gardenias to loving our first, sweet, little grandflower, Lily. With great effort, Steve and I turned most of the space that once was my extensive English flower garden into a soft carpet of lawn to accommodate the little feet that needed a place to run and play.

I remember the first time I invited my granddaughter into my flower world. As we were planting a flat of purple petunias, I took the opportunity to teach her a lesson that, if heeded, could not only save her from a lifetime of regret but could guarantee a lifetime of blessing. I taught her the "laws of sowing and reaping."

As the sun was shining down on us that beautiful late-April day, I said, "Lily, pay attention to the kind of flower we're planting today. We don't plant petunias and grow marigolds. No, the seeds that are planted will be the harvest that is grown." That truth was easily comprehended, even by a sweet three-year-old girl.

As time has passed and Lily is quickly approaching her teen years, I hope she'll remember the importance of considering what she's planting in the garden of her life. If she sows good seeds, a good harvest will be enjoyed. If she sows seeds of rebellion and sin, her harvest will be disappointing...even deadly. Here are two universal truths about reaping that I hope Lily absorbed:

- You reap what you sow.
- You usually reap *more* than you sow.

With great hopes that my grandchildren will be careful when sowing seeds so their harvests will always be good ones, I earnestly pray...

For My Grandchildren

Heavenly Father, help my grandchildren understand that in this life there will always be seedtimes and harvesttimes. Let them know that their job is to plant good seeds so they will grow and bring forth a bountiful harvest that will bless them and not harm them. Help them to sow seeds of righteousness so they will reap a harvest of steadfast love.

As You break the fallow ground in their hearts, please rain down righteousness on them. You've warned that those who plow iniquity and sow trouble will reap the same. The one who sows injustice will reap calamity. For this reason, I ask You to guide my grandchildren so they'll avoid the terrible harvest of wrong that comes from planting sin in their gardens.

> sow kindness and reap friends
> sow generosity and reap prosperity
> sow patience and reap peace of mind
> sow obedience and reap trust
> sow mercy and reap mercy
> sow forgiveness and reap being forgiven
> sow the fruit of the Spirit and reap love
> sow right thinking and reap right living
> sow discipline in what they eat and reap strong,
>   healthy bodies
> sow exercise and reap fitness

Lord, I pray my grandchildren will avoid sowing seeds that will bring devastation and distress to their lives. Help them guard against...

> sowing laziness and reaping poverty
> sowing infidelity and reaping a broken home
> sowing crimes and reaping punishment
> sowing disobedience and reaping consequences
> sowing unbelief and reaping hell

Father, I want all these things for my grandchildren so they'll be beautiful flowers in Your garden that bring You joy.

In Jesus' name, amen.

Genesis 8:22; Job 4:8; Proverbs 22:8; Jeremiah 17:10;
Hosea 10:12-13; 2 Corinthians 9:6-8

17

Working for the Lord

I pray that my grandchildren will
find purpose in their work.

Working in Ministry

Because Annie and I have been in music ministry since the mid-1970s, and because our children were such a visible part of our work for so long, people often ask, "Are your children in the ministry now?" Sometimes when the inquirers come to the words "in the ministry," they use a certain tone of voice that indicates they're actually asking, "Are they music ministers, pastors, on staff at a church, or missionaries?"

When we detect this tone we immediately assume that if we respond with "No," our answer is going to disappoint them and leave them wondering what we did wrong as parents. So we usually ask, "What do you mean by 'ministry'?" If their answer confirms what we suspected, we typically answer, "They're not on staff at a church or on the mission field, and they don't travel and sing Christian music, but they are in ministry."

If we see puzzled looks on their faces, we know our reply requires more explanation. To elaborate we usually add, "Our son, Nathan, is a music producer in Nashville. His light for Jesus shines where he works. He's married to a believer who also performs and works in the music industry. Our daughter, Heidi, is a full-time homemaker. Her light for Jesus shines within her family and when she uses her design skills at church. Her husband's faith shines in his role as vice president and CFO of a large company and in his work as a lay leader at their church. Even more important, our son and daughter and their spouses are in full-time ministry parenting a total of five children (so far) whom Annie and I gratefully call our GrandChaps!"

We hope our answer satisfies the inquirer's curiosity, but more than that we hope we've helped him or her see that "ministry" doesn't always involve a church building or working with indigenous people in a distant land. Being an ambassador of God's gospel of grace happens wherever believers are. This is a truth we want to pass on to our grandchildren too. Wherever they land in terms of their work, God wants to use them in that place to accomplish His will here on the earth. "Joe's Garage" illustrates this truth.

Joe's Garage

If I need some work done
On my '57 Dodge,
I know where I'll be headin'—
Down to Joe's Garage.
Lord knows I can trust him;
He does everybody right.
It's been that way ever since the day
He first saw the light.

He can fix a Chevy; he can fix a Ford.
While he's tuning up your engine,
He'll be talkin' 'bout the Lord.
You won't see pews or stained glass,
Just a man who loves his God
While he's servin' the Lord on a mission field
Called Joe's Garage.

I won't forget that morning
I was drivin' into town.
My old truck started smokin'
I had to shut her down.
Somebody stopped to help me,
Said, "Give old Joe a call."

That's when my soul and my pickup both
Got an overhaul.

Now God may never call you
To the other side of the earth.
But, like Joe, you can tell about Him
Where you live and where you work.[5]

For My Grandchildren

Lord, help my grandchildren see that the time they invest in their jobs isn't wasted if it brings honor and glory to You. Their jobs—whether in the home, at an office, or in the field—can be a ministry when they do it for You. Please show them that the work they choose to do is an opportunity You've ordained. Encourage them to do their work heartily for You and not for bosses and the other employees.

I want my grandchildren to be strong and healthy so they can work and provide for themselves and the people who depend on them. I don't want my grandchildren to yield to the temptation to be lazy because You offer many stern warnings concerning that snare. You warn that lazy hands cause poverty, but the hands of the diligent make them rich. You caution that if the sluggard doesn't plow in autumn, he'll have nothing at harvesttime. Lord, guide my grandchildren so they'll take these warnings to heart.

I know there are those who can't work because they're unable to do so physically, mentally, or emotionally. They need the help of people who are able to work. You've shown us through Your Word that by working hard we can help the weak and affirm the words of Jesus, who said, "It is more blessed to give than to receive."

Whatever work my grandchildren find to do, help them do it with all their might. Give them wisdom so they can provide for their families and share with those in need.

I pray in Jesus' name, amen.

Colossians 3:23; Proverbs 13:4; Proverbs 10:4; Proverbs 20:4; Acts 20:35; Ecclesiastes 9:10

18

Finding Their Song

*I pray that my grandchildren will always
appreciate the value of Christ-centered music.*

Making Melodies in Their Hearts

Steve's and my grandchildren come from a long line of musicians, poets, and performers. It's natural that they were exposed to music and learned to communicate through it very early in their lives.

When our eldest granddaughter was just three years old, Steve took her into our studio, and the two them recorded a Christmas CD featuring her vocals accompanied by Steve on the guitar. He made copies of the disc, and she gave them out as Christmas gifts. The next year Steve did the same, but the recording included Lily's newly acquired skills on the violin. Now the other grands have joined in on the musical experience by taking lessons and performing. As more little ones come along, I'm sure they too will find their unique musical expression and join the band.

Before Heidi got married and gave us three of our wonderful grandchildren, she recorded an album for our independent record company, S&A Family Music. She sang 10 songs written prior to 1900. The accompaniment included nature sounds. Her children have heard this CD as their lullaby music since they were born. I can only imagine how deeply the timeless lyrics of those lovely old hymns are nestled in the nooks and crannies of their spirits.

Music offers a wonderful way to express hearts of worship and praise. It's also a great tool to teach spiritual concepts and stories from the Bible. Through the years, Steve has written songs tailored for our children and grandchildren. What joy to see the next generation learn the wonderful truths of God's Word through lyrics such as "The Silver Dollar Song," which features the parable of the lost coin (Luke 15:8-10).

The Silver Dollar Song

Just suppose a woman had ten silver dollars then
She discovered one of them was missing.
Would she be happy with nine? Oh no, she'd take her time
And search until she found the dollar that was missing.

She'd light a lamp and sweep the house,
look around and search about
Until she found the missing dollar.

Now when she found the dollar,
Do you know what she would do?
She'd make a call to all her friends and neighbors.
She'd be so happy she would holler,
"I found my missing dollar,
Now everyone rejoice with me!"

Now every boy and girl who gives their heart to God
Is like the silver dollar that was missing.
There's joy all around, the day that you were found.
There's joy in the presence of the angels.

Hallelujah, there's joy in the presence of the angels.
You've been found! There's joy among the angels. [6]

I long for my grandchildren to enjoy music that builds up their character and teaches them godly principles. And when they're older, I hope they'll remember with joy the words and melodies they learned by singing with their Grandpa and Grandma Chapman. So I'll continue to pray...

For My Grandchildren

Dear Lord, thank You for the gift of music. When King Saul was troubled in his mind, You sent David to play skillfully on the harp and sing soothing songs that helped quiet the king's spirit. Please use music in the lives of my grandchildren to bring them calm and draw them closer to You. Thank You so much for the talents and abilities You've given them. Show them how to be good stewards of Your gifts and develop them to their fullest potential. Teach my grands to speak to one another in psalms and hymns and spiritual songs. Let them sing new songs and make melodies in their hearts to You.

I know You enjoy music, Lord, for Your servant David and all of Israel played music before You with all their might. They sang and played harps, lyres, tambourines, cymbals, and trumpets.

I pray too, Lord, that You will be the strength and song in the souls of our grandchildren. You are all they need. You are their salvation. Be the night song for my grandchildren in those times when they're troubled and can't sleep. Calm their fears. My wish is that You will take delight in them, and they'll rejoice over You with joyful songs. You are their God.

Give me wisdom in how to encourage them to use their musical talents to exalt and bless You all the days of their lives.

In Jesus' name, amen.

1 Samuel 16:23; Ephesians 5:19; 1 Chronicles 13:8; Exodus 15:2; Proverbs 11:20; Psalm 100:2; Psalm 40:3; 1 Chronicles 16:9-10

19

Honoring God and His Name

I pray that my grandchildren will
honor God always and guard against
using His name inappropriately.

Hallowed Be God's Name

My first six years of formal public education were in a three-room, country school. To complete the final six years required by West Virginia to graduate from high school, every day I (Annie) had to hop on a big, yellow school bus and ride 30 minutes to Central Junior High in a nearby town. One of my favorite classes was physical education, and my favorite teacher was the coach who taught it. Although I wasn't very skilled in team sports, I made up for lack of talent by using brute force. One of the greatest lessons I ever learned in life was taught to me in gym class.

I'm not sure exactly when or why I began to do it, but during sports activities I started cursing—frequently using God's name in a less-than-reverent manner. Whether it was to fit in with the crowd or simply parrot what I was hearing others say, it didn't take long before the careless language became a habit.

One day my gym teacher took me aside and confronted me about my disregard for the name of the heavenly Father. She said, "Did you know that you're breaking one of God's commandments when you use His name like that?"

I was totally embarrassed by my teacher's needed but gentle rebuke. I remember feeling such shame and humiliation. From that day until now I've never forgotten her challenge, and I've never misused God's name again.

These days, if teachers challenged a student to a higher standard of verbal conduct based on a moral cause, they would be putting their jobs at risk. Looking back to the 1960s, I have a feeling that even a threat to my coach's reputation wouldn't have deterred her from correcting my character-damaging habit of abusing God's name. To this day, I thank God for that teacher's courage in helping me straighten out.

I pray my grandchildren will continue to honor and keep holy the name of their Creator, Father God. Thankfully, their parents are careful to help them do just that by restricting the use of words that even hint at using God's name in disrespectful ways. In their families, words like "gee" and "gosh" are off-limits, as well as text abbreviations, such as "OMG." These are considered substitutes for God's name. It not only takes daily training for the children to understand how sacred the name of God is, but it takes a lot of prayer for them to stand tall as they face the temptation to let down their guard when it comes to honoring God and His name. For that reason, I pray…

For My Grandchildren

Dear Lord, I come to You with embarrassment and sadness over the ungodly way Your name is used in our world.

I sincerely pray that my grandchildren will never use Your name in any way except in worship and praise and conversations with You. Remind them of Your holiness and sovereignty. You warn us in Your Word that You will not hold guiltless the ones who take Your name in vain. I pray my grandkids will regard You and Your name with the reverence and deference You deserve. Reveal to them Your very presence so they'll understand and know to give You all adoration, all glory, all praise, all majesty. I want them to be the kind of worshipers You desire, the ones who worship You in Spirit and in truth. Hallowed be

Your name, O God. May it be respected, revered, and honored in every way by my grandchildren.

In Jesus' name, amen.

Matthew 5:33-37; Jeremiah 14:14; Matthew 16:16-17; Exodus 20:7; Matthew 7:21-23; John 4:23-24; Psalm 59:17

20

Depending on Jesus

I pray that my grandchildren will
boast only in Jesus and
His sacrifice on the cross.

Nothing Compares to Knowing Christ

I could spend a long time pointing out to my grandchildren all the things they shouldn't boast about. From having the most popular doll to the latest electronic gadget, from owning the most recent style of tennis shoes to snagging a top role in a stage play, from earning a trophy to being elected class president, but nothing—*absolutely nothing*—compares to the honor and joy of knowing Christ. Along with their parents who are careful to often remind them of this reality, I hope the following song lyric encourages them to remember that as well.

If I Boast

If I boast...it'll only be in the cross
Of the One who died for me
     before I ever knew I was lost.
No other honor could ever be greater than
Knowing the One who made that kind of sacrifice.
So if I boast, it'll only be in the cross of Christ.

Through the cross I lost interest in the things of this world.
And the world has lost interest in me
'Cause I have put my trust in nothing I have
     or nothing that I've done.
It's in the blood...the blood of Calvary.

Oh, Satan is defeated.
The victory has been won.
The only thing I can glory in,
Is what the Lord has done.[7]

For My Grandchildren

Dear God, may it never be that my grandchildren would boast except in the love and sacrifice Jesus Christ made on the cross for them. Through the cross of Jesus, the world has been crucified to them, and they to the world. Let my grandkids boast only about this: that they understand and know You. Help them realize that You are the God who exercises kindness, justice, and righteousness on the earth. May they delight totally in You.

I want my grandchildren to proclaim that knowing Jesus Christ is their biggest achievement and joy. That His sacrifice for them is their foundation for everything they believe, do, and profess. That His life within them is what gives their lives hope, meaning, and direction.

In Jesus' matchless name I pray, amen.

Galatians 6:14; Jeremiah 9:24; 1 Corinthians 2:2; Galatians 2:20

21

Developing Self-Discipline

I pray that my grandchildren will
learn to exercise self-control.

The "Nutty Buddy" Challenge

For quite some time now, Monday has been the day when two of
our homeschooled granddaughters come to our house to stay overnight. While at our house, Steve teaches their art class and, later, I take
them to afternoon violin lessons. What happens often after their music
class is worth noting since it provides a very good illustration of what
it means to have self-control.

When music lessons are over, the teacher rewards his students with
sweet treats. Usually it's a couple pieces of wrapped bubble gum, a pair
of Tootsie Rolls, some type of hard candies, or sometimes all of them.
My grandchildren carry their instruments and treats to the car, get in,
and buckle up. As I start the motor, I wait for the question I know will
be asked.

"If we eat any of our treats from Mr. Dan now, will we still get a
Nutty Buddy at your house?"

(A "Nutty Buddy" is a scoop of vanilla ice cream covered with chocolate and bits of peanuts that sits in a very tasty waffle cone.)

I find it amazing that my grade-school-aged grandchildren know
to ask such a question. It tells me they're discovering how to process
making big decisions—in this case, one that isn't so easy for a child.
They've learned that Steve and I are sugar-intake-sensitive, so they realize they may have to choose between eating the candy in their hands

at the moment or waiting 20 minutes for the frozen treat that awaits them in the freezer when we get back to the house.

In all the Mondays they've left music lessons and faced such a monumental decision, there's been only a few times when they haven't chosen to wait for the Nutty Buddy. Not many kids their ages are so self-controlled.

How thankful I am that their parents are teaching them the incredible importance of self-discipline. This virtue will benefit them through all their coming years and have a far-reaching, positive physical and spiritual impact. To help them continue to develop this life-building, even life-saving attitude, I pray…

For My Grandchildren

Dear Father, help my grandchildren guard against letting short-term temptations derail the self-control that will help them achieve their goals. Guide them in understanding that a person who has self-control is more powerful than a person who can capture a city and that a person who lacks self-control is like a city whose walls are broken down.

Show me how I can teach my grandchildren that Your grace is available to them so they can exercise self-control by saying "no" to ungodly choices and worldly passions. Give me opportunities to teach them that without self-control they can make themselves physically and spiritually sick. I want my grandchildren to know You personally, God, so that through You they'll have everything they need to live a godly life. For this reason, I ask You to help them add goodness to their faith; and to goodness, knowledge; and to knowledge, self-control; and to self-control, perseverance; and to perseverance, godliness; and to godliness, mutual affection; and to mutual affection, love. I know if they possess these qualities and grow in them, they'll be effective and productive in their knowledge of You and in life. This is what I pray for my grandchildren.

In Jesus' name, amen.

1 Corinthians 9:25; Proverbs 16:32; Proverbs 25:28; Titus 2:11-14; Proverbs 25:16; 2 Peter 1:3,5-8

22

Exploring Their Gifts

I pray that my grandchildren will
discover and develop their God-given talents.

The "Artchery" Teacher

The book of Matthew includes a story about investing wealth. Even though this parable doesn't reference anything about singing or playing an instrument, that didn't keep a music director at one church from using the reference to chide an unwilling choir member for refusing to sing a solo in the Christmas cantata. He said to her, "God doesn't want us to bury our talents."

Whether the use of the passage was an errant interpretation of the word "talent" or just a play on words on the part of the music director, there's some merit in how he used it in reference to musical ability. The truth is, not only is it important that we not bury any abilities we might have, but we should also be busy mining our abilities to find what we might otherwise miss.

I (Annie) don't need to go far to provide my grandkids a good example of someone who had a yet-to-be-discovered talent that was uncovered and put to good use. I can point them to their Grandpa Chapman. In his senior year of high school, Steve's creative writing teacher, Mrs. Margaret Withrow, gave her students an assignment one day that broke the ground where a songwriting gift was waiting to be mined. She said to the class, "I want everyone to come back tomorrow with a poem."

Late that night, Steve, who was 16 years old at the time, wrote his first song. It was titled "Psalm 91:7," and featured a story about a soldier whose life was spared when a bullet hit him in the chest. Instead of piercing his body, the bullet was stopped by a Bible that was in his shirt pocket. It was a Bible that his mother had sent him in the mail. Using a melody that resembled the theme song of the then-popular TV show "Gilligan's Island," Steve set the story to music. The next day he sang his composition to the class, and the rest is history. He's been writing story songs ever since.

I like to point out to our grandkids that Steve's songs are more than just entertainment. They have a purpose. They've been used by God to literally change the course of people's lives. Songs like "The Secret Place," which encourages honesty with God, can lead to healing. "You're the Only Little Girl" has been used to strengthen father/daughter relationships. More recently, "Father, Save My Father" expresses the cry of a son praying for the salvation of his dad. These songs are just a few of the products from Steve's discovered talent.

I'm confident that waiting in the minds and hearts of my grandchildren are talents that can also be used by the very One who gives them. Steve and I both want to do our parts to help them discover those gifts. To accomplish that goal, we take part in their homeschool experiences. For the most part, our participation takes place on Mondays during the regular school year. As we've mentioned, I usually take them to their music lessons. Steve, who is also an artist, teaches them art for an hour. When the weather and time permit, he also teaches them archery. We call him their "artchery" teacher.

We don't mind the expenditure of time, energy, and resources required to, as Steve puts it, "mine their minds." We know the return on our investment will be great. In fact, it's already yielded a great return. We hear it when Lily plays the violin or Josephine plays the mandolin. We see it in their drawings and paintings that cover Steve's office wall. Assisting our grandkids' parents in uncovering our grandchildren's gifts that can be used for God's glory is something we take seriously. That's why I pray...

For My Grandchildren

Dear Father, I thank You for the many talents and abilities You've given to my grandchildren. Help them discover what those gifts are, and grace them with the discipline to develop their giftings to their fullest potential. Give me wisdom to do my part as their grandparent. I want to support my grandchildren, assisting them in being faithful stewards of what You've given to them.

Encourage my grandchildren to use their talents, not to bring attention to themselves or have others build them up, but as a means to serve You and others. You've said that a gift opens the way and ushers the giver into the presence of important people. When that happens for my grandchildren, remind them to use those opportunities to bring glory to You.

In Jesus' name, amen.

1 Peter 4:10; 2 Timothy 1:6-8; Proverbs 18:16

23

Sharing Jesus

I pray that my grandchildren will
not allow anything or anyone to silence
their witness for Jesus.

We Won't Be Still

I (Steve) was in a grocery store with two of our grandchildren. We'd gathered the few items we'd gone there to get and were standing in the checkout aisle. A lady came in behind us, and when the kids turned and saw her, they both greeted her with a smile and a friendly, "Hello. Jesus loves you!"

The lady smiled in return and said, "Well, thank you. I needed to hear that today."

I was amazed at how much boldness and sincerity was shown by the two little ones. And I was impressed with how quickly they seized the opportunity to tell people that the Lord loves them. It inspired me to consider my own willingness to be a witness to the people around me.

When I recall the confident look on the faces of my grandkids and the engaging sound of their voices as they spoke about Jesus to a total stranger, my heart swells with grandfatherly pride. But I also have another emotion that I face. My heart aches with the reality that we live in a world that has a fast-growing disdain for mentioning the name of Jesus and what He represents.

To most Christians who live in America, it's obvious that references to God are being systematically removed from the public platform. And this is happening even though our forefathers considered God the foundation on which our nation was built. The evidence is found in the growing absence of His name in schools, media, government, and even some religious organizations.

As our society and the world at large continue to deliberately reject the name of Jesus, it takes growing boldness for those who are His followers to speak of Him openly. Sadly, that challenge has already been faced by one of our grandkids. It happened in her second-grade classroom at a public school. An assignment was given by a substitute teacher for the students to write down their answer to this question: "Who do you want to be most like when you grow up?" Our granddaughter answered simply, "Jesus." When the teacher saw her answer she whispered to our little grandwitness, "You can't use that name here." Our granddaughter was devastated by the teacher's response, and the effect on her young faith was significant.

With these types of stories becoming more and more common, I wrote the following lyric to encourage my grandkids and other believers in Jesus.

We're Gonna Talk About Jesus

Peter and John were on their way up to the temple
When they prayed in Jesus' name and God healed a cripple.
But the elders and rulers didn't like what they did so they
    jailed 'em
And said don't use that name around here—it's not welcome.
But they said...

Chorus
We can't stop talkin' 'bout Jesus; there's just too much to tell.
And He's the One who came to save us, and He made
    that cripple well.
You can put us on trial for saying the name of
    the One who died to redeem us.
Do what you will, but we can't be still.
We're gonna talk about Jesus.

After two thousand years it appears not much is different
'Cause the name of Christ still offends, and many
    don't want to hear it.
Even our makers of law want us all to be quiet,
But just like Peter and John, we won't be silent.[8]

My hope is that the melody and the words of this story from Acts, chapters 3 and 4 will echo in the minds and hearts of our grandchildren so when they get older and face even more opposition they'll proudly keep proclaiming the name of Christ.

It's for their sakes and for the sake of the precious name of Jesus that I pray…

For My Grandchildren

Heavenly Father, I bring my grandchildren to Your throne asking You to be their strength when they are called to be Your witnesses. In those times when they're asked to give an account for the hope that is in them, I know You'll give them the words they need. Help them tell about You with gentleness and respect, keeping a clear conscience before those who might slander them and treat them maliciously.

I know it's through the blood of the Lamb and the word of their testimony about You that the enemy is defeated. Give them confidence to speak out. Provide the courage they need to not deny You, Jesus. For if they endure for You, they will reign with You.

Lord Jesus, all authority in heaven and in earth has been given to You. Grant Your blessings to my grandchildren so they will, wherever they go, make disciples for You, baptizing them in the name of Your Father, in Your name, and in the name of the Holy Spirit. I pray all these things knowing You will be with them, even to the end of the age.

In Your name, amen.

Matthew 10:18-20; 1 Peter 3:15-16; Revelation 12:11; John 1:1-5; John 16:33; 1 John 2:13-14; John 17:20; 2 Timothy 2:12; Luke 12:8-9; Matthew 28:18-20

24

Slaying Envy and Jealousy

I pray that my grandchildren will
avoid the fierce jaws of envy and jealousy.

Two Monsters

It's a tradition the girls and their grandpa looked forward to from one year to the next: birthday dress day (BDD). When their birthdays came around, the hunter instinct came out in PaPa. As though he was preparing to bag another record-book deer, he cleared his schedule, scoped out the stores for the best selections, and planned for the trek up the retail mountain called "the mall." The hunt was on for that special granddaughter dress or, as the girls call it, their "PaPa dress."

Under the adoring and approving eye of their grandpa, much time and attention were given to the selections offered as they browsed the racks in the stores. Of course, finding the garment was only a small part of the outing. No dress is complete without a pair of shoes or a hair ribbon to go with it. Maybe a little purse or matching stuffed animal is needed to complete the ensemble. And, without a doubt, shopping creates a strong hunger for a soft pretzel, cone of ice cream, or both.

So how did such a fun day turn into a red-faced, tear-stained, I'm-not-getting-out-of-the car experience for our eldest grandgirl? Because it wasn't her birthday. It was Josie's big day, so Lily was going to stay at our house and wait for her sister and PaPa to return.

I (Annie) was at the house when Lily and her mother came over after school, but Lily wouldn't get out of the car. She'd learned that Josie and her PaPa were about to leave for their "PaPa dress" outing, and she was upset. Concerned because she was feeling bad, I went out to the van that was parked in the garage.

"Why are you still in the van?" I asked. All the other times Lily had been invited to tag along on Josie's BDD, but now that Josie was getting older it was time for her to have her special time with just PaPa. I could see Lily's downcast countenance and was sympathetic toward her struggle. Being the eldest has its advantages, but it also has a particular disadvantage that has to be faced at some point. Sometimes being the firstborn means identifying with the old saying, "Pioneers take the arrows; settlers take the land." Being the first to knowingly have to stay home while her sibling got to go with PaPa was hard. I reasoned with Lily to help her see the situation wasn't as unfair as she believed.

"Did you get to go with PaPa on your birthday while Josie had to stay home?"

"Yes, but Josie didn't care because she was little."

I smiled gently as I responded, "I understand. Tell me what you're feeling."

Through pursed lips, Lily was quick to answer. "I'm just a little hurt."

"Hurt?"

"Yes, my feelings are hurt that I don't get to go with Josie and PaPa."

I put my arm around Lily. "You're not hurt, sweetheart. You're jealous and envious. You need to call this what it is. Jealousy in this case is wanting what someone else has, and envy isn't wanting them to have what they have. Did you know that when you're jealous and envious of someone it means you aren't loving them?"

"That can't be true. I love my sister!" Lily protested.

"The Bible tells us that love isn't jealous. Love doesn't envy. Love wants what's best for the other person. And do you know what else, Lily?"

"What, DeDe?"

"We actually *choose* to love one another."

Lily gave me a puzzled look. "How can I do that when I don't feel loving? I feel mad and angry that I don't get to go on the shopping trip."

"I understand. I too have to fight the temptation to be unloving and selfish. But love is much more than how we feel at the moment. Love is an action, an attitude, and, perhaps the most important, love is a *decision*. Can you go tell your sister that you're happy for her? Can you tell her that you choose to love her and want the best for her? Can you tell her you are choosing to not be jealous?"

Lily answered softly, "Could I work on my attitude while she's gone? I'm not quite ready to smile and be happy. But I am ready to try to do it."

"Yes, of course you can work through this while she's gone. But when you start to get angry and selfish again, when the two monsters called jealousy and envy want to come back into your heart, you can think of right now when Josie went with PaPa for her birthday dress day and you decided to act loving toward her. Doesn't that sound like a good thing to do?"

"Yes, I can do that," Lily replied. And with that she got out of the van, and we went into the house.

I was amazed at how understanding and accepting Lily was of my challenge to embrace the truth about jealousy and envy. While the experience wasn't easy for her to work through, by the end of the evening Lily was in good spirits. When the next year rolled around, I was even more surprised at how differently she handled staying home while her sister went on her annual hunt with her PaPa. Lily's supportive and very sweet demeanor that she displayed as her sister and grandpa left the house told me she'd received my message about the "two monsters." She now knows that if they're allowed to dwell in her heart, they'll be "love killers" and make her miserable. This is a lesson that will serve her well for the rest of her life.

Knowing that the "Birthday Dress Day" challenge won't be the only opportunity for my granddaughters to do battle against the two monsters, I pray…

For My Grandchildren

Dear Father, peaceful hearts give life to the body. But when the damaging jaws of envy and jealousy appear, chaos reigns. Deliver my grandchildren from those two monsters. Grant them discerning spirits so they'll know when these two monstrous deeds of the flesh are lurking. Please help them understand that where there is jealousy and selfish ambition there is also disorder and evil practices.

Set a seal on the hearts of my grandchildren that will keep out evil. Give my grands the will to rid themselves of all wickedness, deceit, and envy. Only You can protect them from this trouble. Put in their hearts the desire to grow in You. Strengthen them so they'll be blameless and holy in Your presence. Fill them with love so there will be no room for anything as destructive and unbecoming as envy and jealousy.

I pray this in Jesus' name, amen.

Proverbs 14:30; Philippians 1:9-10; James 3:14-16; Song of Solomon 8:6; 1 Corinthians 13:4; 1 Thessalonians 3:13; 1 Peter 2:1-3

25

Living Without Secrets

I pray that my grandchildren will
live all their days with nothing to hide.

The Attic

At the time of this writing, my parents are nearing their nineties. I
(Steve) am extremely grateful that both of them have been around to
meet their great-grandchildren. They've even been blessed to hold a
great-great-grandchild born into my sister's family.

Of all I can tell my grandkids about their great-grandparents, I'm
extra pleased to tell them that my folks are two of the best examples
they'll ever know when it comes to how people can live rightly before the
Lord. While there are many virtues I could mention, there's one quality
they possess that may especially inspire my grandkids to live with a higher
moral and spiritual standard. That virtue is having nothing to hide.

I realized that my parents had no secrets to conceal when I was at
their house one day. Mom needed something out of the attic. At their
age, if they can avoid climbing the pull-down ladder in their hallway,
they will. Since I was there to drop the ladder and make the climb, they
asked me to do it.

There wasn't a whole lot of stuff in the space, but it was my job to
rummage through the cardboard boxes and plastic storage bins to find
what they needed. As I did, this thought came to me: "If there was
something up here either of them wouldn't want me to find, they never
would've asked me to do this." I smiled at the thought of what an open
book my parents' lives are.

I'm convinced that living secret-free lives is one of the reasons they've enjoyed so many wonderful years. Not constantly worrying that someone might find something that would embarrass them or damage their good name yields a peace that undoubtedly has contributed to their good health physically and spiritually.

The peace of mind that my folks have known as a result of having nothing hidden that would haunt them is something I want to have. I don't want to instantly break into a sweat when my grandkids come to our house and I find them rummaging through a chest of drawers or exploring our attic (which they love to do). I prefer the contentment that comes with having nothing that I dread they might uncover.

I know that someday, if the Lord tarries His coming, I'll only be a memory in the minds of my grandkids. In regard to the way I want to be remembered and the influence my life might be on those I love—especially my grandchildren—the following song lyric says it best.

Nothing to Hide

The day had come to go through our grandpa's things—
Pocketknives, old black and whites, and his wedding ring.
When our work was finished and no stone was left unturned,
What we all suspected was confirmed.

He had nothing to hide,
Nothing to hide.
His house was just like his heart—no question marks inside.
The best gift he ever gave
Is written in stone on his grave.
He lived the way he died;
He had nothing to hide.

On my way back home it occurred to me,
I still have time to leave that kind of legacy.
So I gave the Lord my secrets; don't want to leave behind any wrong...
So my family can say when I'm gone,
"He had nothing to hide."[9]

For My Grandchildren

O Father in heaven, I know that a great accomplishment for me as a grandparent would be that I could say to my grandkids as Paul said to the believers in Corinth, "Be imitators of me, as I am of Christ." For that reason, help me show my grandkids what it means to allow You to search my heart to see if there is anything that is not pleasing to You. I thank You for the blessed hope that when Christ appears I will see Him as He is. That hope compels me to do all I can to purify myself as He is pure.

I pray for Your help to live with nothing to hide, and I also want this for my grandchildren. Give them wisdom to understand that nothing is hidden from You, and that one day they will stand before You and be required to explain all they've done. You'll bring to light what is hidden in darkness and expose the motives of their hearts. At that time, their decision to live free of dark secrets will yield the joy of receiving Your praise.

May their years within the framework of time be spent free from sin so that when they step out of time and into eternity, they will praise You because Your Son, Jesus Christ, was their support to keep them from stumbling. Through Him they will stand blameless in the presence of Your glory and experience joy in You.

In Christ's name I pray, amen.

1 Corinthians 11:1; Psalm 139:23-24; 1 John 3:2; Romans 2:5-6; 1 Corinthians 4:4-5

26

Representing Their Faith

I pray that my grandchildren
will be good citizens.

Part of the Solution

Every generation before us has made the necessary sacrifices to assure the next generation had a better shot at the American dream than they had. To our national shame, that forward-looking attitude seems to have ended with the "Baby Boomers" (those born between 1946 and 1964). Never before has one generation saddled the next with such incalculable debt, geopolitical decline, and moral degradation.

Many of us remember a time in our country when the future seemed much brighter. We were proud of what America stood for in the world. Now we look back and shake our heads in perplexity at how so many things have changed. Some can, however, look back without regret that at least they did their part to make our nation a better place.

My first recollection of being involved in the political process was during the presidential campaign in the fall of 1960. I (Steve) was attending Beech Hill Elementary School in Southside, WV. I'd just turned nine years old. During lunch hour and at recess, while the other children played on the playground, I would take my homemade political sign and stand by the highway in front of the school. I wanted to voice my First Amendment right to free speech through cardboard and crayons. No one told me to do it; it was something I desired to do. Even at nine years old it seemed important that I participate in the national decision-making process.

In November of that year, my dad and I stayed up well into the night waiting for the election returns to come in. As it turned out, West Virginia would play a pivotal role in the outcome of the 1960 presidential election.

Fast-forward to January 2014. I can happily report that the grand-apple doesn't fall far from the grandtree. Lily, at age nine, was invited, along with the rest of the 8- to 12-year-old homeschool students of Tennessee, to participate in a learning program called TeenPact, which centers on the political process, the value of liberty, and how to engage in the culture. She and her dad spent the day at the Tennessee State Capitol.

Throughout the day Lily learned about running the state, parliamentary procedure, and the various agencies that keep our state functioning. She participated in a "pretend session" on the floor where state representatives pass laws. She managed to stop the passage of the imaginary bill with her dissenting vote. "Go, girl!"

What a great opportunity for these young people to get their "public-service feet wet" by learning how our state operates. Another fun part of the experience was meeting and talking to some of the elected officials.

Tennessee's secretary of state was speaking with Lily and her father, Emmitt. The secretary said to our very poised Lily, "Someday you may have my job."

Without missing a beat, Lily looked him straight in the eye and said, "Actually, I was thinking more on a federal level." When that was reported to me it brought a huge smile to my face. After her dad told more of the story of Lily's conversation with the state dignitary, I commented, "Actually, I think a nine-year-old could do a better job than the ones in office right now on the federal level."

Whether our granddaughter settles for being governor of Tennessee or president of the United States, it doesn't really matter. Whether she lives in a regular house taking care of her family or in the White House taking care of our nation, what's important is that she sees herself as part of the solution and not part of the problem. I desire to see my grandchildren be productive, good citizens for our country. I want them to make a real and lasting difference. That's why I pray...

For My Grandchildren

Dear Father, I thank You that I'm privileged to live in the United States and raise my children in freedom. Although it grieves me to see our nation's moral decline, I know You have a plan for this world. You are in charge, and nothing can alter that fact. Until You come and set up Your kingdom on this earth, I want to be Your light and salt in this world. I desire that for my grandchildren as well.

I pray my grandchildren will keep Your light burning in the world they occupy. As today's culture grows darker and darker, may their lights shine brighter and brighter. I know a lighthouse doesn't blow its own horn; it just stands and shines. In times ahead, if my grandchildren are in a position where they can't speak out for You, may the inextinguishable light of Christ shine in and through them. Give them courage to stand up and stand firm—even if they have to stand alone—for what is pleasing in Your sight.

Even the fleeting thought that my grandchildren might have to suffer any degree of emotional or physical pain is almost more than I can bear. However, I know that many of Your children have suffered in the past, and some are suffering now for the sake of the gospel of Jesus Christ. If my grandchildren are called to sacrifice for the cause of Your Son and for doing what is right, I pray they will do so without fear.

Through Your strength, help them choose Christ as their Lord and Savior. In those times when they're called on to give an account for the faith they hold dear, grant them the wisdom and responses that will be life-bearing to those around them. May they do so in gentleness and respect, keeping a clear conscience so those who speak maliciously against them will be put to shame for their slander. Comfort them and remind them they are privileged to share in the sufferings of Christ.

Father, I know You've called my grandchildren to righteousness. You promise to hold their hands. Keep them firmly in Your care. Thank You for not leaving them in darkness so they can be prepared when trials occur. They are Your sons and daughters—children of Your light. They don't belong to the darkness. As children of the day, may my grandchildren help preserve this land and delay the rotting effects a godless culture can have on the moral fabric of this world. I pray they will courageously stand for the sanctity of life, the unchangeable truths of the Bible, the God-centered and God-ordained family unit, and the propagation of the gospel of Jesus Christ.

Surround my grandchildren with Your love. Uphold them and keep them safe until You come again. Even so, come quickly, Lord Jesus.

In Your name I pray, amen.

Job 38; Proverbs 16:9; Ephesians 1:11; Matthew 5:13-16;
Psalm 18:28; 1 Peter 3:13-16; Isaiah 42:6; 1 Peter 4:12-13;
1 John 1:5-7; 1 Thessalonians 5:4-8; Matthew 28:18-20;
John 17:15; Revelation 22:20

27

Giving Away God's Compassion

*I pray that my grandchildren will show
compassion without judgment.*

God's Love in a Parking Lot

To encourage our grandchildren to offer compassion to people without passing judgment, there are some excellent examples from the life of Jesus to draw on. For instance, He fed 5000 hungry people with just a few loaves of bread and a couple of fish, He raised a widow's only son from the dead, and He healed two blind men (Matthew 14:15-21; Luke 7:13-15; Matthew 20:30-34). He wasn't responding to their moral behavior when He stopped to talk with them. Instead, He was focused on their needs. If He'd waited until they reached a perfect state of spirituality before helping them, none of the miracles would have taken place.

As a grandparent, I (Annie) long for our grandkids to know that it pleases God when Christ's unconditional compassion is still being shared today. One example I've used to help our grands know what it means to be a conduit of compassion involves a story about a young couple Steve and I know.

This couple was out on a date. After they left the restaurant they got into their car to head home. They drove through the parking lot and noticed a woman standing by the opened trunk of her car holding a red, plastic gas can. Because it appeared she was having some trouble, they pulled up beside her. The husband opened his window and asked, "Do you need some help?"

The woman answered, "We're passing through town and ran out of gas, but someone helped us get this gallon so we could at least get to a gas station. Thanks so much for asking."

The young couple noticed there were children in the backseat of the car, and that the inside was filled with personal belongings. Guessing the woman and her children were living in the vehicle, the husband asked, "Do you need some money?"

Tears instantly formed in the woman's eyes.

The couple pooled their cash and gave the lady almost $50. They received heartfelt thanks and drove away, but they didn't leave the area. They went to an ATM machine, withdrew more cash, and returned to where the woman was still parked. When the couple pulled up and gave the extra money to her, they heard the children squeal with excitement. The couple decided the kids were excited about the possibility of some hot food and maybe a comfortable hotel room for the night.

The young couple didn't ask the woman why she was homeless. They didn't ask her if she was using drugs or drinking, if she was divorced, if she knew who fathered her children, if she was abused, if she was running from the law, or any other personal questions. All they did was respond to a need that a desperate woman and her children obviously had. The young couple gave compassion without regard to the receiver's moral state or situation.

I realize people need to be very wise when offering assistance to those in need so people won't take advantage of them or, worse, cause them physical harm. However, withholding compassion from the destitute because of distrust can cause people to miss opportunities to be God's hands of goodness and, ultimately, miss openings to share His love for them.

As my grandchildren learn more about the importance of showing compassion to others without passing judgment, and as they seize occasions to do so, I continue to pray...

For My Grandchildren

O, merciful, compassionate God, You show great kindness to us even though we don't deserve it. Indeed, You're gracious and compassionate, slow to anger and rich in love. What a delight to put my trust in You!

You ask us to follow Your example by showing mercy to those who doubt You, by rescuing those heading for negative judgment, and by offering mercy even as we carefully avoid the sin that contaminates their lives.

I pray my grandchildren will seek to be like You by showing mercy and not judgment toward those who are needy. Though the one in need may be caught in some sinful web or tangled in an encumbrance that weighs them down, help my grandchildren not entertain thoughts of rebuke and judgment. You, Lord, are the only one qualified to judge. Encourage my grandchildren to trust You and let You take care of that because You are holy and just. Your mercies are new every morning. Great is Your faithfulness.

Instill a compassionate and tenderhearted attitude in my grandchildren, especially toward the needy because we're all destitute in one way or another. Just as Your kindness leads them to repentance, may Your great mercy lead my grandchildren to compassion. Give them opportunities to help people with their time, resources, and listening ears.

Father, because today's world is filled with evil people who find pleasure in devising ways to hurt others, please give my grandchildren discernment when it comes to showing compassion to those who look like they need a hand. Show my grandkids how to recognize the trickery of takers who want to harm people. Keep them from getting discouraged and overwhelmed by the number of people who could use assistance and the con artists.

When an opportunity does arise to show compassion to someone who needs assistance, regardless of his or her spiritual state, help my grandchildren resist the temptation to assign motives and condemn the people. Remind my grands that they too were once weak and in need of redemption. Let them not become weary in doing good, but encourage them to do good to all people—especially to the family of believers in You.

In Jesus' name, amen.

> Romans 5:8; Psalm 145:8; Jude 22-23; John 8:7-11; Lamentations 3:22-23; Romans 2:4; Matthew 19:21; John 12:5-6; Hebrews 12:1-3; James 2:1-2; Galatians 6:1-2; Galatians 6:9-10

28

Praising God No Matter What

I pray that my grandchildren
will experience real joy despite
any difficult circumstances.

"Hallelujah Coming from the Valley"

Our grandchildren's great-grandmother Lillian Chapman (Steve's mom) is probably the most positive person I know. Though she's suffered much since her teen years from the effects of a back injury, and she's now dealing with the ailments that go with being in her senior years, she seems to always have an optimistic outlook. I especially notice when I call her. I ask, "How are you doing, Lillian?" Her reply is usually a good-natured, "Well, I'm doing real good for someone in my condition!"

I'm very grateful for the encouragement I get from my mother-in-law's answer. It inspires me to keep the same upbeat perspective. And I'm also very thankful that our grandkids (Lillian's great-grands) are blessed to know her and glean from the joy that comes with her consistent, positive attitude. But, as Lillian admits, it's not always an easy way of life to maintain.

Steve and I watched Lillian deal with grief due to the loss of her parents, seven of her eight brothers, one of her two sisters, her mother- and father-in-law, three brothers-in-law, and two sisters-in-law, all of whom she loved dearly. We've seen her wrestle with the stress and grueling emotions that come with being a pastor's wife. And we've observed her as she prayerfully stands by many of her friends who are fighting cancer and other life-threatening diseases. Through it all she raises her hands and gives God thanks and praise for His goodness.

One time when Steve's songwriting friend Jeff Pearles came to our house, he brought an idea for a song about praise. As Jeff and Steve wrote the lyrics, Steve kept his mom's face in mind because she represents what this lyric says better than anyone he knows.

Hallelujah Coming from the Valley

There's a sound God can hear
Oh, it's music to His ears.
Rising on the wings of a hurting heart,
Past the mountains to the sky,
Climbing to His throne on high...
He hears a "hallelujah" coming from the valley.

And it tells Him
One of His children
Found the will to praise Him
Where it seems all hope is gone.
And it tells Him
They'll be leaning...
Leaning on His grace to keep moving on.
Oh, how He loves to hear a "hallelujah"
Coming from the valley.

Oh, dear child, is it true?
You're the one who's walking through
That place where you fear you're all alone?
Lift your voice and let it swell
'Cause your praise is where He dwells.
He's in your "hallelujah" coming from the valley.[10]

I sincerely hope that I can be as joyful in the face of hard circumstances as Lillian Chapman has been and still is. I desire this not just for myself, but also for the sake of our grandchildren. I want them to see that God is honored when He's trusted, and that no matter how deep the valley, if they believe He's with them and hears their cries, it will be pleasing to Him. With this hope in my heart, I pray...

For My Grandchildren

Father God, I want my grandchildren to know that even though they will face difficult situations in their lives, they can still experience Your amazing peace. That peace is possible because neither death nor life, neither angels nor demons, neither the present nor the future, nor any powers, neither height nor depth, nor anything else in all creation, can separate them from Your love sent to them through Your Son, Jesus Christ our Lord.

Strengthen my grandchildren with Your power according to Your glorious might so they will have great endurance and patience when the circumstances of life leave them hurting. Show them how and why they can give thanks with hearts full of joy to You in every situation. Even though weeping may last for the night, assure them that comfort and rejoicing comes in the morning. Thank You for being with them always.

Father, give my grandchildren the grace to consider it pure joy when they face trials. Give them wisdom to understand that the testing of their faith, even though it may not feel good at the time, produces positive things, including perseverance. My confidence is in You—that You will mature their faith so my grandchildren will be mature, complete, and lacking nothing.

In Jesus' name, amen.

Philippians 4:7; Romans 8:38-39; Colossians 1:11-12; Psalm 30:5; James 1:2-4

29

Planning for the Future

*I pray that my grandchildren will
find good and godly mates.*

The Two Shall Become One

It was Lily's turn to pray first. Josie had gone first the last time we said our nighttime prayers together. From the top bunk I heard my granddaughter sweetly praying. There was the usual request for the Lord to bless and keep all her family members healthy and happy. She was careful to pray for Pastor Sam and all the folks at church. And she always remembered to include Gregory and his family. He was the child their family supported through a Christian food ministry.

As her adorable voice continued to list all of her blessings and concerns, my attention was fully engaged when I heard her pray these words, "And, dear Father, bless our future husbands and help them to be godly young men. May their parents teach them to love You and serve You. And, Jesus, please help our parents teach us to be godly young women who will love and serve our husbands and take good care of the families You give us." As she continued to pray, I could almost hear the words coming from the hearts of her parents, who had prayed this blessing over them since they were tiny babies.

Of all the decisions our grandchildren will make, after choosing salvation through Jesus, the choice of mates will be the one that will have the most impact on their lives. I pray my grandchildren will choose godly mates who love God and hate sin.

But that's not all. While loving one another is essential for a *successful* marriage, "liking" one another and "being likable" are also essential if they're going to have *happy* marriages. The words Steve penned for me on our thirty-eighth anniversary say it well.

I Like You Too!

I love you—you know it's true.
It's one good reason why I married you.
But that's not all, just one more thing
That makes me glad I asked you, would you wear my ring?

I like you too.
I really do.
No one else treats me quite as nice as you.
In every way,
I have to say,
You're the dearest friend I ever knew.
Oh, I love you, babe…
And I like you too.

Oh, I love you more than life itself!
Oh, I love you more than a million words could ever tell.

And I like you too.
I really do.
No one else treats me quite as nice as you.
In every way,
I have to say,
You're the sweetest friend I ever knew.
Yes, I love you…
And I like you too.[11]

With hopes that my grandkids will know this kind of love, I pray…

For My Grandchildren

Heavenly Father, in Jesus' name, I join with my children and grandchildren as they pray about their futures. I pray that Your will—Your good, pleasing, and perfect will—becomes their hearts' delight. Please give them wisdom and guard them against becoming involved with people who don't know You. Guide them to someone whose highest ambition is to please You so they'll enjoy strong relationships that honor You.

Even before they meet their mates, I ask You to help them stay physically pure and teach them what commitment means so they'll be ready to be wholly dedicated to the one they will someday be joined with in a covenant marriage. Put a hedge of protection around them to keep those who would take advantage of their affections far from them.

For my granddaughters, I ask that You would help them become noble women of character. I pray that their husbands will see in them women who are worth far more than rubies. I pray that my granddaughters will respect their husbands and be the helpers You want them to be.

For my grandsons, I ask that You help them become men after Your own heart. I pray that they would recognize that the man who finds a good wife is very blessed. He receives favor from You. Show them how to love and cherish their wives even as Jesus loves His church. Guide them as they lead their families in confidence and put their full trust in You to assist them in carrying out their responsibilities.

Lord, be with my grandchildren and their spouses so they can enjoy all that You intend marriage to be for them. May they feel deep love and commitment to one another. I want them to relish their sweet companionship because they know they are divinely connected to the mates You ordained to be their best friends.

If it is Your will that my grandchildren marry, I ask You to help them experience the great mystery of a husband and wife becoming one in heart, mind, and body. Only You, heavenly Father, can create such a lasting bond. And with Your seal of approval and participation, I know that not even the gates of hell can separate two people You've joined together.

In Jesus' name, amen.

Proverbs 18:22; 2 Corinthians 5:9; 2 Corinthians 6:14; Proverbs 31:10-12; Genesis 2:18; Ephesians 5:28-33

30

Embracing Marriage

I pray that my grandchildren will
be faithful to their spouses.

Faithfulness

The reports of great harm done to relationships as a result of unfaithfulness are always sad and discouraging to hear, but it is especially impacting when the people involved are in the national spotlight. This might be true because the weight of the consequences that come about due to sinful choices are felt more significantly by the masses. Very possibly this is the reason God included David's adulterous affair with Bathsheba in the Old Testament.

When it comes to the issue of infidelity, the serious rippling effects include the debilitating despair that fills the soul of the devastated spouse, the emotional scars on the children, financial consequences, torn reputations, and the ongoing loss of trust. Oh, how I hope that our grandchildren will never know the intense pain caused by the serrated edge of the dividing knife of adultery. For that reason, I pray...

For My Grandchildren

Marriage is Your idea, dear Lord, and it is indeed a wonderful plan. Long before the Ten Commandments were given to the Israelites, long before any government authority was established, and long before the Christian church was born, there was the concept of marriage. I pray my grandchildren will respect, honor, and keep holy the sacred and ancient covenant of marriage.

I pray that the marriage bed my grandchildren and their spouses enjoy will be kept undefiled and exclusive. Keep each couple safe and guard the individuals against becoming adulterers or sexually immoral.

You've told us that from the beginning You created mankind male and female. And that a man will leave his parents and join with a woman to create a new union based on Your design. You've united the two into one, and what You join together, no person should separate.

Encourage my grandchildren to listen closely to the wisdom in Your Word and have good sense when it comes to remaining faithful to their spouses. The words of the immoral may be sweet and smooth, but the result of being unfaithful to a spouse is bitter poison and pain. I don't want my grandchildren to follow depraved people and be led down paths that lead to destruction. Therefore, I ask You to help them remain true to You and to their spouses. With Your assistance they can remain pure and totally committed to their mates and families.

Help my grandchildren be faithful in all ways. You've charged them in Your Word to be that way, and that if they're faithful in little ways, they can be trusted in more important matters. Please give them the strength to walk with You and be totally Yours.

In Jesus' name, amen.

Hebrews 13:4; Matthew 19:4-6; Proverbs 5:35; Luke 16:10

31

Trusting God's Love and Grace

I pray my grandchildren will
know and understand God's grace.

"Do You Love Me When I Do Wrong?"

A friend shared a conversation she had with her granddaughter Lauren, who learned a truth I (Annie) want my grandchildren to know too.

Lauren was busy picking up the DVDs that were scattered across the den floor. Her grandmother had told her several times that if she failed to put the discs back "into their houses" after she was finished watching them, they would get scratched and no longer play. As hard as Lauren tried, it was just too easy to take a disc out of the player, put a new one in, and not put the first one away.

When her grandmother walked into the room, she looked at her granddaughter's hurried efforts to cover up her negligence.

"What did I tell you, Lauren? I'm not going to buy you any more DVDs if you don't take care of the ones you have."

The rebuke from her grandmother was the last thing Lauren wanted to hear. She loved her Grandma very much. Lauren was sorry that once again she'd disappointed her. With a slight whisper, Lauren asked fearfully, "Grandma, do you love me when I do wrong?"

Her grandmother stopped and looked straight into her eldest granddaughter's beautiful, hazel eyes. "Yes, Lauren. I love you even when you do wrong. In fact, I think I love you even more because I can relate to you. You see, I do wrong things too. My love for you has nothing to do with your behavior. *I love you because you are mine.* And do you know what else, Lauren?"

"No, Grandma."

"God loves you when you do bad things too. He knows how much we need Him."

Hearing that statement, Lauren paused in her work.

Her granddaughter's silence cued Grandmother that she needed to explain what she'd just said. "Lauren, can you see my underwear?"

The shocked look in Lauren's eyes brought a smile to Grandmother's face. She asked the question again. "Can you see my underwear?"

"No, Grandma!"

"Why not?"

"Well, it's because you're wearing blue jeans and a sweatshirt."

Grandma took her granddaughter's hand and looked her in the eyes. "Young lady, you're exactly right. You can't see my underwear because of what I have on over them. This is a picture of what happened when you asked Jesus to come into your heart. When you surrendered your life to Him, God clothed you in a robe of righteousness. And when God looks at you now—and me too—He no longer sees our 'dirty underwear' of sin. Instead, He sees the clean, beautiful garment of salvation called Christ's righteousness. That's what grace is all about. Grace is God choosing to see Christ who covers us instead of the bad we've done."

Steve and his friend Jeff Pearles wrote a beautiful song that can benefit tender ones like Lauren. In fact, it was written especially for one of our grandchildren.

I Still Love You

In those times when I stumble,
    and I know I've done wrong,
The shame leaves me feeling so alone.
And I start to wonder,
"Did I sin His love away?"
But what a sweet assurance
When I hear His voice of grace…

I still love you!
I still love you,
Even though I know you well
And I see you when you fail.
Even when your darkest secret is revealed,
Be still and know I'll never let you go
'Cause I still love you.

When I feel so unworthy,
    and I'm drowning in regret,
He whispers, "You're forgiven, and child,
    don't forget…
I still love you."[12]

It's taken me nearly a lifetime to comprehend God's far-reaching grace, and I'm still trying to fully grasp its immensity. My hope is that it won't take my grandchildren as long to understand it. I know that accepting God's grace will affect every aspect of their lives in such meaningful and positive ways. That's why I pray…

For My Grandchildren

Dear Father, of all I could ask on behalf of my grandchildren, one of my greatest desires is that they understand that You love them and Your love *is not* conditional. I want my grandchildren to know they can't be good enough to be found acceptable in Your sight and, on the flip side, they can't be bad enough to be rejected by You. Oh, what grace You give!

Help me show my grandchildren that sin will have no dominion over them in You because they're not under law but under grace. Encourage them to walk by the Holy Spirit so they will not gratify the desires of the flesh. For by Your grace my grandchildren will be saved through faith, and not by their own doing. Salvation through Your Son Jesus is a gift from You! Your grace leaves no room for anyone to boast.

I pray that my grandchildren will know in their hearts that they've been released from the law. They've died to that which held them captive. Now they can serve in the new way of the Holy Spirit and not in the old way of the written code. Father, make it clear to my grandchildren that they can't be justified by trying to follow a set of rules. It's impossible. Instead, reveal the beautiful redemption and grace You provided through the finished work of Your Son, Jesus Christ. You are such a wonderful God!

Assure my grandchildren that because of Jesus they can live free from condemnation, for the law of the Spirit of life has set them free in Christ Jesus from the law of sin and death. In Jesus my grandchildren have redemption! Through His blood, they will experience forgiveness of their trespasses according to the riches of His grace. Thank You, Father.

In Jesus' name, amen.

Romans 6:14; Galatians 5:14; Galatians 5:4; Ephesians 2:8-9;
Romans 7:6; John 3:16; Romans 8:1-2; Ephesians 1:7

32

Seeking Truth

I pray my grandchildren will
embrace truth and reject lies.

Be a "Truther"

One day my grandchildren were playing in the next room. I (Steve) heard one of them accuse the other of having told a lie. The rapid and earnest response of the accused rang in my ears: "I'm not a liar! I'm a truther!" Even as I smiled at the exchange, I knew I wanted my grandchildren to understand the importance of telling the truth to and about others. But even more importantly, I wanted my grandchildren to be on guard to the lies they might tell themselves.

One of my greatest desires for my grandchildren is they will learn, believe, and speak of the certainties that are found in God's Word. Without this foundation of truth, falsehoods and deceptions will surely take root and eventually take over. There are a couple of things my grandchildren can do to be free from the prison made from wrong thinking and careless speaking.

First, they must take every thought captive. Instead of being a *prisoner* to the lies of the enemy, they must become the *guard* so they can put those negative, discouraging thoughts in solitary confinement. Without food (dwelling on them, giving them credence), the deceptions will die.

Second, they must replace the lies (now in solitary confinement) with the truths found in the Word of God. Here are just a few common lies our enemy (Satan) uses to deceive.

- *Lie:* Guilt over past sin. *Truth:* God never brings up sins that have been confessed and forgiven. God chooses to not see those sins because they're covered by the blood of Jesus (1 John 1:9; Ephesians 1:7, Hebrews 9:14; Colossians 1:13-14).

- *Lie:* Thoughts of not being good enough. *Truth:* My grandchildren are holy and without blame before God through Jesus Christ. It's not their goodness that matters—it's Christ's (Ephesians 1:3-5).

- *Lie:* My grandchildren will go to hell when they die. *Truth:* They are sealed with the Holy Spirit. It's not what they've done or will do that counts, but the finished work of Jesus on the cross that guarantees heaven (Ephesians 1:13-14).

- *Lie:* No one loves them. *Truth:* They are fully accepted and loved by the Father. He has lavished His love on them through and because of the redeeming work of Jesus on the cross (1 John 3:1).

I will faithfully and continually ask for wisdom and discernment as I pray…

For My Grandchildren

Father in heaven, with a grateful heart, I praise You for defeating Satan, the father of lies, who wants to deceive my grandchildren. Please deliver them from being conformed to this world's way of thinking. Instead, encourage them to let Your Word renovate their minds. In that way, they'll prove what is the good, acceptable, and perfect will of God.

Fill their minds with what is honorable, right, pure, lovely, and of good repute. And if there is anything excellent or worthy of praise, let their thoughts dwell on it.

Help my grandchildren, O Lord, set their minds on things above, not on the things that are earthly and temporal. In those times when they're struggling and feel under attack, help them to remember that their struggle isn't against people or situations but against the enemy of our souls. The best weapons with which they can fight against the devil are prayer and Your Word wielded in the power of the Holy Spirit.

I pray in Jesus' name, amen.

John 16:11,33; Luke 10:18; John 8:44; Romans 12:2; Philippians 4:8; Colossians 3:2; 2 Corinthians 10:4-5; Ephesians 6:12,17-18

33

Adapting to God's Timing

*I pray my grandchildren will understand
that there's a time for everything.*

A Time To...

The well-known "time for everything" passage in Ecclesiastes starts with, "There is an appointed time for everything. And there is a time for every event under heaven" (Ecclesiastes 3:1-8). There are everyday examples we can use to help our grandkids understand that there is indeed "a time for every event under heaven." Here are a few ideas.

- " a time to give birth and a time to die" (verse 2): a new puppy replaces a longtime pet that died
- "a time to plant and a time to uproot what is planted" (verse 2): tending a vegetable garden
- "a time to tear down and a time to build up" (verse 3): an old barn is torn down so a new one can be built
- "a time to weep and a time to laugh" (verse 4): attending a funeral; going to a funny movie
- "a time to throw stones and a time to gather stones" (verse 5): skipping rocks at a lake
- "a time to keep and a time to throw away" (verse 6): helping with a family yard sale
- "a time to be silent and a time to speak" (verse 7): in church; in Sunday school

- "a time to love and a time to hate" (verse 8): a sibling; a sin

I want my grandchildren to understand God's timing, so I pray...

For My Grandchildren

Father, help my grandchildren understand that You've set times for all of life's events, and it's to their advantage to embrace Your timing for each one. Show them that because You've set forth a proper time and procedure for every matter, You can be trusted with everything that pertains to life, whether it be a burden or a blessing.

Lord, I pray especially that You will remind them that just as You set the seashore as the limit for the waves to travel, so also You have set a time when they too will travel no more in this life, and after that they will face judgment. By Your saving grace, and that alone, will they be ready for that moment.

In Christ's timeless name I pray, amen.

Ecclesiastes 8:6; Proverbs 8:29; Hebrews 9:27

34

Admiring God's Handiwork

*I pray that my grandchildren will
see God in His handiwork.*

Evidence of the Divine

Steve is an avid outdoorsman. He often says, "I even like mowing the yard. I welcome any excuse to be outside!" His specific interests are hunting and fishing. While our family often enjoys the tasty benefits of his trips to the woods and waters, our grandchildren receive a special benefit from their granddad's love of God's great outdoors. Whenever he can, Steve points to something in creation that speaks of the Creator in an effort to help the kids know and appreciate who God is.

Steve wrote this lyric to reveal the truth that God does indeed exist and He is great.

It's in His Nature

When evening light begins to fade
And rolls back the curtain of the day
To reveal the stars on an endless stage
I see His glory.
It's in His nature.

When I'm standing on the shore,
Where rocks and waves fight their wars,
And I hear their mighty voices roar,
I feel His power.
It's in His nature.

In the woods, in the fields,
I look around and know He's real.
And I feel the touch of Someone greater.
I can see His love for me.
It's in His nature.

When I see a spotted fawn,
At a mountain stream at the break of dawn,
Drink until its thirst is gone,
I see His goodness.
It's in His nature.

In the shade of the summer leaves
That saves me from the burning heat,
I think of yet another tree,
And I see redemption.
It's in His nature.

In the woods, in the fields,
I look around and know He's real.
And I feel the touch of Someone greater.
I can see His love for me.
It's in His nature.[13]

Because I too believe God has given mankind—including our grandchildren—plenty of evidence of Himself, I pray...

For My Grandchildren

Almighty God, Maker of heaven and earth, Your invisible qualities, Your eternal power and divine nature, have been clearly seen, being understood through what has been made, so that people are without excuse. I pray my grandchildren will enjoy Your great outdoors and see who You really are. I want them to know You better because of it. Let my grandchildren know that through You all things were made; without You nothing was made that was made. For in You all things were created: things in heaven and things on earth. The visible and the invisible, whether thrones or powers or rulers or authorities; all things have been created through You and for You. You are before all things, and in You all things hold together. Knowing this, I hope my grandchildren will not only understand who You are, but they will also more fully trust You because of Your greatness.

When my grandchildren gaze at the skies at night, turn their thoughts to You and that You alone are God. The heavens, even the highest heavens, and all their starry host, the earth and all that is on it, the seas and all that is in them declare Your majesty. You give life to everything, and the multitudes of heaven worship You. Please allow my grandchildren to add to the sweet refrain of worship.

As nature is moved to worship, so let my grandchildren worship too. Let the heavens rejoice, let the earth be glad; let the sea resound, and all that is in it. Let the fields be jubilant, and everything in them; let all the trees of the forest sing for joy. Let all creation rejoice before You, Lord. When my grandchildren have questions about creation, may they turn to Your Word and understand You, Mighty God, are the Maker of all.

In Jesus' name, amen.

Romans 1:20; John 1:3; Colossians 1:16-17; Nehemiah 9:6; Psalm 96:11-13

35

Guarding Against Pornography

I pray my grandchildren will avoid
the devastating effects of pornography.

Play, Little Boy

When I (Steve) was around seven years old, I had an encounter that had the potential to destroy my life. What took place is similar to the story written in this lyric.

Play, Little Boy

She said, "Little boy, while your daddy's at work
We'll go see my friend. Go put on your shirt."
He said, "While we're there, Mama, what can I do?"
She said, "I know they have a little boy just like you...

"And you can play, boy, play.
Play, little boy, play.
It'll be a nice way to spend your day.
You can play, boy, play."

Two mamas talking; two busy boys.
And it didn't take long to get tired of the toys.
"My daddy hides some pictures,
     and I've found them before."
Two innocent eyes hide behind a door...
     where they have

Playboy, play.
Play, little boy, play.
And the devil does his part to steal
    another young heart.
With *Playboy,* play.

That night his mama kissed him and
    they said his prayers.
He wanted to tell her, but he was too scared.
She said, "By the way, did you like your
    new friend?
Maybe someday soon we'll go back again...
    where you can...

"Play, boy, play.
Play, little boy, play."
But how could she have known what
    sorrow was sown
With *Playboy,* play?
Have mercy, O Lord, on all the boys in the world
Who have *Playboy,* play.
Have mercy, O Lord, on all the dads in
    the world
Who have *Playboy,* play.[14]

There are lots of ways that grandchildren might encounter pornographic images. A peer might show them explicit photos or others may find magazines that a dad, an uncle, a brother, or a grandfather assumed were well-hidden. Some might inadvertently be exposed via unexpected and unsolicited pop-ups on a computer monitor or late-night TV. Whatever the source of the images, whether deliberate or not, the experience can imprint on young minds like a brand burned into the hide of a steer.

The negative results on children's lives that pornography cause are well-documented. It destroys their innocence, it distorts their view of the godly beauty and intent for the opposite sex, and it can lead to insatiable desire for more perverted material. Although I've specifically mentioned boys, it's true that girls also get introduced to pornography with the same deadly effects. This danger is enough reason to go before God to earnestly pray...

For My Grandchildren

O mighty Father in heaven, I pray that You will guard my grandchildren so they won't be exposed to the dangers of pornography. Your Word says "the eye is the lamp of the body. If your eyes are healthy, your whole body will be full of light. But if your eyes are unhealthy, your whole body will be full of darkness." I ask You to surround my grandchildren with Your protection and put adults in their lives who will watch over them and shield their eyes from evil.

Guard my grandkids' eyes so they won't see material that is worthless and designed to destroy their innocence and corrupt their hearts. Create in them a thirst for all that is noble, pure, lovely, admirable, and of good reputation.

And, Lord, when they're older, encourage them to depend on You to avoid enticements. Remind them there is no temptation that can overtake them if they depend on You and Your faithfulness. Thank You for always making a way of escape for them so they would be able to endure it and overcome it. Open their eyes to the battle that is raging around them, and let them see that You're fighting with and for them. They are never alone.

Show my grandchildren the way to flee from sexual immorality. Every other sin a person commits is outside the body, but sexually immoral people sin against their own bodies. O Lord, I pray my grands will keep pure hearts, for out of the heart flows everything they do. I desire that they will know that You, Lord Jesus, came to proclaim liberty for the captives and recovery to the blind and to set at liberty those who are oppressed. Please do this in the lives of my grandchildren.

In the name that is above all names, Jesus Christ, I come against the powers of darkness that want to render my grandchildren captives to the god of this world. You, Father in heaven, are the one true God. You have already defeated the enemy of their souls. You've set my grandchildren's feet on solid ground and given them armor for the battle against darkness. Encourage them to live in the confidence of those truths.

In Jesus' name, amen.

Matthew 6:22-23; Luke 11:33-34; Psalm 101:3; Philippians 4:8; 1 Corinthians 10:13; Philippians 4:8-9; 2 Kings 6:17; 1 Corinthians 6:18; Proverbs 4:23; Luke 4:18; Philippians 2:9; 2 Corinthians 4:4; Ephesians 6:13

36

Making God Their Refuge

I pray that my grandchildren will
know the comfort of the Holy Spirit
in times of sorrow.

My Deep Sorrow

How I (Annie) made the drive back to my in-laws' house in one
piece that night is still a mystery. Looking back on my state of mind,
I shouldn't have been operating a vehicle. Part of me was in complete
shock and denial, but another part knew exactly what had just happened. Standing at my mother's bedside with the rest of my family, I'd
just witnessed my sweet mama completing her last task. She'd made
the arduous journey from this life to the next.

As I walked through the unlocked back door of the house where I
was staying, I was relieved to find it empty. After all that had happened,
I desperately needed some time alone with the Lord.

As I wept from the pain and grief of such a gut-wrenching loss, my
heart sensed the presence of the Lord. I began to feel His peace that
surpasses all understanding washing over my wounded spirit (Philippians 4:7). What I'd anticipated was complete devastation; but what I
was experiencing was the comfort of the sweet Holy Spirit. My uncon-
trollable sobs eventually turned into prayer. "O, Father, I've trusted You
with my whole life. I know I can trust You to take care of my mama."
That's all I could say. And I'm confident that it was enough. In times
when sorrow washes over us like a relentless tsunami and tries to wipe
out the foundation of all we know for certain, the Holy Spirit comes
alongside us to be our constant comforter.

I earnestly hope my grandchildren will know where to go in those times of deep despair so they'll realize they are not alone. For this cause, I pray…

For My Grandchildren

O Father, what a comfort to know that even when my world seems to be falling apart, You're always here for me. I know You'll always be here for my grandchildren too. In this world I know they'll face tribulations. They'll experience heartbreak and trouble. I praise You that they can be of good cheer because You, Lord Jesus, have overcome the world. Please let my grandchildren know beyond all doubt that You are their refuge and strength, a very present help in trouble.

I hope my grandchildren will humble themselves under Your mighty hand, O God, that You may exalt them in due time. Cares of this life are much too heavy for their mortal shoulders. As they cast their cares on You, may they feel the reassurance that You care for them. I know that because of Your great love we are not consumed, and it's all because Your compassions never fail. In fact, Your lovingkindness is new every morning. Great is Your faithfulness!

You don't despise or abhor those who are having a hard time. The affliction of those who are afflicted is not hidden from Your face, but You've heard them as they cry out to You. I love You, Lord, because You've heard my pleas for mercy on behalf of my grandchildren. Because I know You hear me, I will continue to call on You as long as I live. Weeping may last through the night, but joy comes with the morning. I pray my grandchildren know that. Help them to see how much You care about them. I know You keep track of their sleepless nights, and You've collected all their tears in Your bottle. I'm amazed but not surprised at how much You care for my grandchildren. Give them the courage to proclaim throughout their lives that You are good. You are a stronghold, a place of protection and refuge in the day of trouble. You take note of those who choose to make You their hiding place.

One more thing I ask on behalf of my grandchildren. Encourage them to seek after You. Shelter them in the day of trouble. Conceal them under the cover of Your tent and establish them on a firm foundation so that when the waves of sorrow wash over them, they'll stand firm on Your rock.

In Jesus' name, amen.

John 16:33; Psalm 46:1; 1 Peter 5:6-7; Psalm 22:24;
Psalm 116:1-2; Lamentations 3:22-23; Psalm 30:5; Psalm 56:8;
Nahum 1:7; Psalm 32:7; Psalm 27:4-5

37

Protecting Their Faith

I pray my grandchildren will
understand that if they stray from the faith
a "posse of love" will come after them.

"Surrounded"

When our two eldest granddaughters were old enough to travel
with me, I (Steve) planned an adventure trip with them that yielded
some great memories—as well as a very important spiritual lesson.
Our first stop was in the Cincinnati, Ohio, area to go to the Creation
Museum. It was a great place to take the grandkids because it's packed
with interesting information, ideas, and hands-on activities. There are
life-size and miniature dioramas (from the time of dinosaurs to Noah
building the ark), a movie presentation, interactive displays, petting
zoos (including an opportunity to ride a camel), and much more. (I
heartily recommend it.)

From there we went to visit my parents in Point Pleasant, West Virginia. While in the area, I took the grandkids by the farm where Annie
was born and raised and pointed out the school where she and I met
for the first time.

We traveled on to Chapmanville, West Virginia—yep, named after
my family—and we reconnected with some of my uncles, my only living aunt in the Chapman lineage, and some of my cousins. We went
just a few miles further south to see the hollow where I was born.

Parking at the end of a road that led up the long hollow, we all got
out. I pointed to the area where my Grandma and Grandpa Steele had

lived (my mother's parents). Then I told my granddaughters a story about something that had happened to me when I was a child.

In the fall of 1953, just three months prior to my third birthday, my mom and dad left my sister and me at our grandparents' home while they went away for a week to attend a church convention in Cleveland, Tennessee. I believe it was the fourth morning when my grandparents awoke and realized I was gone.

As my grandfather, grandmother, and my two young uncles looked frantically for me they prayed, hoping I hadn't wandered out to the well and fallen in or found my way to the abandoned coal-mine shaft further up the hollow. They had no idea where I was!

What they didn't know was that I'd decided I'd rather stay at Grandma Chapman's house. I'd gotten up early and headed down the hollow on my way to town. I was intent on walking to Chapmanville where she lived.

Thankfully, I needed help putting my little shoes on right, so I stopped at the next house down the road. The adults at that home knew right away that a little transient wearing a diaper and an undershirt wasn't supposed to be traveling by himself. While one of their boys helped me with my shoes, they sent another one running up to the Steele place to let them know their grandson was being held safely on the front porch until they could come and carry him back home.

With that news, my Uncle Bobby hightailed it to the neighbors' home to reclaim the little runaway. I imagine the panic likely sliced a few years off of the life of everyone in the Steele family who found themselves suddenly involved in an all-out search for me, but other than that, all was well.

After telling my granddaughters my story about heading out and then being recaptured and reunited with my grandparents, I told them something I hope they never forget.

"Girls, if you stray from the faith in Jesus your parents have told you about, I want you to know there's a whole bunch of us who love you enough to search for you until we find you. First there's God the Father, God the Son, and God the Holy Spirit who will be tracking you. And then there will be your parents, your sisters, your grandparents, your aunts, your uncles, your cousins, your church family, and your friends. When we find you, you can count on the fact that you'll be totally surrounded with love, and there'll be no way you can escape!"

After enjoying the area for a while, we all piled back into my vehicle. As I drove out of the narrow hollow where I'd once been a toddling prodigal, I reminded my grandgirls of a song I'd played for them a few days earlier. It was written with my friend Dana Bacon. He'd strayed from the faith when he was a young man but was "recaptured" by those who loved him. I sang the lyrics again to reinforce what I was teaching.

Surrounded

I was running from the Lord,
   running from the light;
Running to the wrong, away from the right.
I was alone in my sin, that's what I thought,
But God moved in, and I was caught.

I was surrounded.
There was no doubt.
I was surrounded;
I had no way out.
The Father, the Son, and the Holy Ghost,
And the prayers of the people who cared the most
For my soul—they wouldn't let me go.
I was surrounded.

It was a battle for my soul, but Jesus won that war.
So I'm staying with Him; not running anymore.
The devil may try to get me back, it's true.
But there's a circle of love that he
   won't break through.

I'm surrounded, there's no doubt.
I'm surrounded, but I don't want out.
By the Father, the Son, and the Holy Ghost,

And the prayers of the people who care the most
For my soul—they won't let me go.
I'm surrounded.[15]

I hope our grandchildren never stray from the Lord, but if they do, they can expect a "posse of love" to pursue them. That's why I pray…

For My Grandchildren

Dear Lord, how thankful I am that You, the Son of Man, came to seek and to save the lost. You did this because You desire that all people be saved and come to the knowledge of Your truth. You know it's my heart's desire that our grandchildren be among those You save, and that they will never stray from the fold of the redeemed. But if they do, let them know in their hearts that if caught in any trespass, we who love them and who lean on the Holy Spirit for guidance will restore him or her with a spirit of gentleness, for we know that we too need mercy.

If any of my grandchildren do stray from Your truth, I pray for Your wisdom in how to turn them back to You. You said that if we do that, their souls will be saved from death and will cover a multitude of sins. Thank You for Your work of redemption and restoration, and thank You for allowing me to be part of Your plan.

Blessed be Your name in which I pray, amen.

Luke 19:10; 1 Timothy 2:4; Galatians 6:1; James 5:19

38

Learning to Be Content

I pray that my grandchildren will
handle their finances responsibly.

Welcome to the Real World

The first two questions I (Annie) asked my granddaughters when I saw them on Saturday afternoon was, "How did the yard sale go?" and "Did you make any money?" From the answers they gave, I was a little surprised at the cheerful attitude they displayed. I knew they, along with their mom, had spent an entire week sorting through clothes, selecting the stuffed animals they were willing to part with, and choosing which toys and books they no longer needed or wanted. Getting everything ready for the sale had been a lot of work. And, in doing so, they'd also created quite a messy house.

On the morning of the garage sale, Steve and I kept the baby of their family, our two-year-old granddaughter, all morning so the two older girls and their parents could take care of the hordes of bargain-snappers that would probably descend on their neighborhood. We'd heard it had been a very busy day, and now I was waiting for the report about their bottom line. The eldest sister spoke up first.

"Fifty cents!"

"Did I hear right?" I wondered. "Is there something wrong with my ears?" I was compelled to probe a little deeper. "How much did you make?" I asked again. This time I added, "Didn't you sell that delicious, white-chocolate Chex mix and lemonade too?"

"You heard me right, Grandma. We made 50 cents each. The ingredients for the Chex mix cost us 40 dollars, and then we had to tithe on our sales. After we paid Mom back and gave God 10 percent, we had 50 cents left—each. Oh, and we gave away the lemonade hoping it would help us sell more of the white-chocolate mix."

Then the younger of the two salespeople spoke up. Her comment explained why they weren't more disappointed with the results from their week's work.

"Mom and Dad shared their profits with us, so, actually, we got 12 dollars each."

Though the yield from their efforts would figure out to be mere pennies per hour, I'm sure the yard-sale lessons my granddaughters learned were worth much more than what they netted. After more discussion, I found out they'd also realized that...

- hard work is rewarded—but not always
- it really does take money to make money—or not
- paying back Mom (the investor) is important
- tithing is a good habit to develop

I'm proud of my daughter, Heidi, for taking the time and doing all the hard work so our two granddaughters could have such a valuable experience with handling finances. All they learned at the yard sale and in preparing for the sale will serve them well in the future. There is so much more about money they'll need to learn. As time goes on, I hope they'll continue to gain wisdom about this very important part of life. That's why I pray...

For My Grandchildren

Dear Father, help my grandchildren learn how to handle their finances responsibly. Money, whether there's plenty or not enough, causes a lot of stress and distraction. No matter how much or how little money my grandchildren make or handle throughout their lives, I hope they'll view wealth through Your wisdom. In Your written Word, You show that people can have plenty of money but not be rich and that we can have many possessions but not be wealthy. True wealth is not having all we want; true wealth is having all we need plus You. Please teach my grandchildren this crucial principle.

Help my grandkids avoid becoming greedy. Jesus said, "Watch out! Be on your guard against all kinds of greed; life does not consist in an abundance of possessions." Greed is an enemy. Solomon, the world's wisest and richest man during the time he lived, said we should honor You with the firstfruits of all our crops. Help my grandchildren understand and heed this wisdom. As a result of this act of love and display of gratitude toward You, I'm confident You will provide all they need. Remind my grandchildren that if they follow Your ways, You will give them the ability to produce wealth. With that wealth please give them contentment so they won't know the sorrow that comes from always wanting more and never being content with what they have. You give the power and strength to earn money. Guard my grandchildren from saying in their minds that it was their own might and ability of their hands alone that was responsible for all they accomplished.

When it comes to dealing with money, please keep deception and lies far from them. Protect them. If having too much will make them forget You, please withhold riches from them. If having too little will distract them from full devotion to You, please give them more. Feed them with the food that is their portion.

Show my grandchildren how to guard against greed and embrace generosity. Give them enough, Father, so they can share with others. Your Word says that You make all grace abound to us, so that we always have sufficiency in everything.

Give them understanding so they'll always be content with whatever they have. I know that contentment is found in trusting You. Please keep their lives free from the love of money, for You've warned that the love of money is a root of all sorts of evil. Help them to never wander away from the faith because of their attention on getting money. I want my grandchildren to put their faith in You—not on the uncertainty of riches. I know You'll generously provide them with all they need—with plenty left over to share with others. Thank You.

In Jesus' name, amen.

Luke 12:15; Proverbs 3:9-10; Deuteronomy 8:18; Deuteronomy 8:11-14; Proverbs 30:8-9; 2 Corinthians 9:8; Philippians 4:11-13; Hebrews 13:5; 1 Timothy 6:10,17

39

Trusting God with Dreams

*I pray that my grandchildren will
be able to withstand the disappointments of life
without blaming God or becoming bitter.*

The Dream House

Maria had lived in the rental house just about as long as she could stand it. No one was more aware of the effect that the economic downturn had taken on the housing industry than she was. The house she and her family had left behind in another city so her husband could take a new job had been on the market for three years before it finally sold at a hefty loss. But as hard as it was to sell their previous home, it was equally difficult to find one to buy that was worth the outrageous price the local sellers were asking.

Maria had been more than patient in the days, months, and now years that she'd lived among the unopened boxes filled with household items. She was more than ready to unpack and put down some roots.

Then, one sunny afternoon driving home from the store, she noticed a house that had just come on the market. Could this be the one? Wait! Was that a halo surrounding that two-story, white, *Country Living* magazine-style mansion? Did she really hear angels singing? Well, no, but it sure seemed like it!

From all appearances this was the house she'd been looking for. The right size—not too big, but big enough. It was a nice neighborhood—not "snobs knob," but very nice. What about the price? Surely it would be out of their range. But no! It was surprisingly reasonable.

Motivated by her find, Marie prayed, "Okay, Lord. Now that I've found it, I'm going to trust You to help us get it!" With excitement she took some pictures with her phone and began dreaming. Next came a quick call to the property agent first, and then to her husband. Within a couple of hours they were walking on the beautiful, hardwood floors. She rubbed her hand across the exquisite marble counters in the kitchen. It was perfect. In her heart, she immediately moved in...lock, stock, and sealed, dusty boxes.

After a long talk with her husband that evening, a quick prayer for guidance and favor, and a check-in with a mortgage company, early the next morning Maria was on the phone with the agent. She was ready to make an offer.

Then the wind left the sails of her ship that was taking her to the residential paradise. She couldn't believe what she was hearing. Much to her disappointment, another couple had been just as impressed with the house and, the evening before while Maria was talking to her husband, had made an offer that the homeowners had accepted. The house was sold.

To say the very least, Maria was devastated. How could this happen? No, how could *God* let this happen? Her heart was heavy with the thought of all those long months and years of living in that cramped rental house continuing on into the future. What a disappointment to find and then immediately lose the house of her dreams.

Every time she drove by that beautiful white house it was like a knife going through her heart. She didn't pray it out loud, but in her mind she protested, "Oh, Lord, why can't I have anything I want? Why couldn't I have that house? It was perfect for us. I'm so disappointed in You."

Then, a few days after the new owners moved in, she drove by the house and saw several trucks parked on the front lawn. Something significant was happening at the residence. She stopped and asked a neighbor across the street from the house what was going on. They told her the house had been built over a snake pit. The exterminators were there to tear out the drywall and remove at least three nests of rattlesnakes from inside the walls. They could only speculate about how many vipers were lurking inside and underneath the house.

Was God being mean to Maria by keeping her from having something she desperately wanted? Or was He looking out for her by withholding something that could have harmed her family physically and financially? Maria knows the answer is that God knew what was best for her all along. She humbly apologized to Him, and from that moment on knew she could trust Him with where they would live, as well as all other facets of her life.

When my grandchildren face disappointment because they didn't get something their hearts were set on, I plan to share Maria's story with them. My hope is that they too will trust God and know that He always has their best interests in mind. So I pray...

For My Grandchildren

In those times when things don't turn out the way my grandchildren hope and they're tempted to doubt Your goodness, heavenly Father, encourage them to trust You. You've proven Yourself faithful and good time and time again. Keep them from being deceived. Every good and perfect gift is from above, coming down from You. You never change; You are good all the time.

Let my grandchildren know beyond all doubt that You work all things for the good of those who love You, to those who are called according to Your purpose. Your Word says my grandchildren can cast their burdens on You. You, my Lord, are strong enough to carry them and sustain my grandchildren. I know You'll never let the righteous be shaken.

Gently guide my grandkids to humble themselves under Your mighty hand, that You may exalt them in due time. I know that casting their cares and their hurts on You is the only way they'll find peace and avoid the temptation to become bitter when life takes unexpected and unwelcome turns. My grandchildren can trust You because You care for them.

I rejoice that the plans You have for my grandchildren are good ones—plans to prosper them, and not to harm them. You have plans to give them hope and a future. I pray they will seek Your face, that they will call on You. In those times when they feel like they can't pray because their hearts are heavy with grief and disappointment, let them feel Your presence even more keenly. I know if they call on You, You will answer them. If they seek You, they will find You. You alone are worthy of their trust.

In Jesus' name, amen.

James 1:16; Romans 8:28; Psalm 55:22; 1 Peter 5:6;
Jeremiah 29:11-14

40

Connecting with Believers

I pray that my grandchildren will
be connected to a community of believers.

Connected

When Annie and I started traveling together as a singing duo in
the 1980s, our children were mere tots. Nathan was three, and Heidi
was less than one. For the next 18 years we spent nearly every week-
end on the road. While Annie and I felt called to the work we were
doing, we knew our lifestyle presented a hazard that was of great concern to us as parents. We worried that our kids weren't a regular part
of a church family.

Though we were sitting together in a pew almost every Sunday, we
knew we wouldn't be there but for an hour or so, and then we'd be
headed to the next church in a different city. Because we were in and
out of places, the friendships our young ones established were brief.
Consequently, they didn't get to know the depth of camaraderie that
the kids at our home church were enjoying. Even when we happened
to be home on a Sunday and went to our church, the kids couldn't
really dig in and be part of a core group because they were there usually only one Sunday per quarter.

The apprehension Annie and I felt regarding the long-term effects
that might come as a result of our children not having roots in a congregation loomed before us like a dark cloud. Still, because we felt
called by God to our ministry, we pressed on with our travels as a family. While we hoped our lack of close connection to a church body

wouldn't yield a terribly negative result in the lives of our kids, we also made it a matter of prayer.

We're happy to report that God's solution to our concern has blessed us beyond measure. It came in the form of our in-laws. After ceasing their travels with us, both our children chose to attend Christian colleges. During that time, they both met their mates-to-be. Our daughter-in-law and our son-in-law grew up attending and being committed to local churches, and each of them carried their desire to be connected to a congregation into their marriages.

Annie and I love hearing our children and their families talk about the depth of fellowship and the close friendships they enjoy at their home churches. We're profoundly grateful that their children are also partaking of the fruit of God's answer to our prayers. Our grandkids tell us about their Sunday school classmates as if they are brothers and sisters. It's a glorious thing for us to hear and behold! And what joy to go to their churches and see them singing and taking part in events like choir presentations and plays.

Our desire for our grandchildren to be attached to a local congregation where they feel welcome and part of the fellowship is based, in part, on our awareness that there is a particular safety that goes along with belonging to a group of like-minded people. The principle I'm referring to is well-illustrated in the animal world. For example, when a caribou calf gets separated from its mother and strays from the herd, the prowling wolves move in and take advantage of the unprotected and vulnerable prey. In a similar way, when God's sheep are out in the world alone, they can become prime targets for every spiritual predator in the area.

I don't want to see our grandchildren suffer the consequences of not being part of a healthy flock of believers in Jesus. Their inner lives are at stake. For this reason, I pray…

For My Grandchildren

You made us to need one another, Lord. That fact was made very clear when, in the garden, You declared, "It's not good for the man to be alone." And through the words of Solomon, You let us know that two are better than one. Some of the advantages of being associated with others is there's greater return on our labor, there's help when we stumble and fall, the cold world feels warmer with two, and there is better safety when we're threatened with harm. It's obvious we're not designed to go through this world alone.

I pray that my grandchildren will be connected to a community of like-minded believers who will help them navigate the rough waters of this life. I want my grandkids to feel the security of knowing the loving support of a church family, especially during times of stress and duress. Being a part of a church family also gives them more opportunities to help others bear their burdens and vice versa.

Encourage my grandchildren to gently spur one another on toward loving and actively helping others. Let them continue to meet with believers so they can encourage and be encouraged in the faith—all the more as they see the day of Your appearing approaching.

In Jesus' name, amen.

Genesis 2:18; Ecclesiastes 4:9-12; Galatians 6:2;
Hebrews 10:24-25

41

Revealing Jesus

*I pray that my grandchildren will live
in a way that points to God.*

Living Proof

Many years ago when our kids were small, I (Steve) would give the parental pre-shopping speech as we prepared to exit our car and enter a grocery or department store. "Kids, when we get inside, I want you to act nice, stay close to me, don't disappear, and whatever you do, don't forget that you represent the Chapman clan!" Basically, my challenge to them was to behave in a way that wouldn't stain our good name. I'm grateful to report that while they weren't perfect, all in all our kids cooperated with the charge given to them.

Enough time has passed now that I hear our children give their children nearly the same speech. Not only has it happened at grocery and big box stores, but I've heard it when I've ridden along with them to a restaurant, to church, or to someone's home for a visit. I'm thankful to be able to say that our grandchildren are doing well with this challenge too.

My hope for them is that the cooperation they're giving to their parents now will carry over to their relationship with God. I'll do what I can to help their parents in this effort. I'll remind my grandkids that they're ambassadors of Christ so they'll know that whatever they do in word or deed will reflect on Him as well as His family. That's why I pray...

For My Grandchildren

Father in heaven, I lift up my grandchildren to You as they progress through their childhood, their teens, and on into adulthood. Please remind them that they're not just children of earthly parents, but because of the blessing of reconciliation through Your Son, Jesus, they also belong to You and Your family. Help them be imitators of You and act as Your beloved children.

May they not imitate what is evil but what is good. Your Word says that the one who does good is of You; the one who does evil has not seen You. Help them walk in love, as Christ loved them and gave Himself up for them. Give them wisdom to avoid foolishness, and filthiness, and crude joking, which are out of place in Your family. May they, instead, find joy in embracing the truth that they're chosen by You and are part of a royal priesthood…a people for Your own possession whose main charge is to proclaim Your excellencies and how You called them out of darkness and into Your marvelous light. May You make them living stones that are being built up as a spiritual house, to be a holy priesthood, to offer spiritual sacrifices acceptable to You through Jesus Christ. Encourage them to always walk in a manner worthy of the calling to which they've been called, with all humility and gentleness, with patience, willing to bear with others in love and eager to maintain the unity of the Spirit. I know if they live in such a way that pleases You, others will want to know You.

In the holy and blameless name of Jesus I ask these things, amen.

1 Thessalonians 1:6; 3 John 11; Ephesians 5:1-2; 1 Peter 2:9; 1 Peter 2:5; Ephesians 4:1-3; 3 John 11

42

Getting Ready for Danger

*I pray that my grandchildren
will always be on the alert.*

An A-minor Attitude

When our young grandkids are at our house and gathered with us in the den, sometimes I (Steve) sneak out and head to our living room. I sit down at the piano and, without warning, suddenly fill the house with music. My favorite choice is an instrumental that is up-tempo and in the haunting key of A minor.

I'm never there to see it, but Annie says that without exception every time the music starts each child gets a startled look on his or her face because the song is a cue to look for a place to hide. While I play, I can hear them running as they scramble to find a spot where they won't be found. I build the tempo and volume as they scurry around. Suddenly I stop the music and yell, "Ready or not, here I come!" Then the fun continues as I roam the house looking for them.

I played this game with their parents when they were small, and what joy I experience to be playing this unique take on hide-and-seek again. Perhaps the only drawback is that for the rest of their lives, whenever our grandkids hear a song in the key of A minor, they might have a tendency to suddenly look for a place to hide. That could be very embarrassing if they're at a symphony concert.

Our music-based version of hide-and-seek is more than a game. It's an illustration I use to teach them an important lesson about safety and readiness. I don't scare them, but I do remind them that at any moment, if they're listening, life can start playing in the key of A minor. When that happens, they'll know it's their cue that something is wrong and they should hightail it to a place of safety. When the warning song starts, that's their cue to run and hide in the shadow of God's wings.

As much as I dread to think about it, Satan really does hate our grandchildren, and his intention is to steal them, destroy them, or kill them. My sincere longing is that as our grandchildren enjoy life, somewhere in the back of their minds is an abiding, A-minor awareness. That's why I pray…

For My Grandchildren

Dear heavenly Father, help my grandchildren know they have a stalker—an enemy, a deceiver—so they must be on guard. The devil goes about like a roaring lion looking for someone to devour. Help my grandchildren know that he can't consume them without their permission and their participation. You warn us in Your Word of the wiles of the enemy. Help them heed those warnings and depend on You for the strength to resist the devil. When they resist, he will flee. Remind them to draw near to You because, when they do, You'll draw near to them. Show them how to be on the alert against the enemy and his wily ways, especially when…

- sin wants to take root in their lives
- wrong beliefs want to get them off track
- people try to deceive and take advantage of them
- people want to do them physical harm
- greed rears its ugly head in any form
- unforgiveness and bitterness try to intrude in their lives

I pray that my grandchildren will not be like others who are asleep and unaware, but that they'll be alert and self-controlled and ready to help others. Guide them so they'll always be ready to respond when the Holy Spirit starts playing in the key of A minor.

I pray this in Jesus' name, amen.

Revelation 12:9,12; 1 Peter 5:8; James 4:7-8; Matthew 16:6-12; 1 Timothy 4:13-16; Matthew 7:15; Luke 21:8; Matthew 10:17; Luke 12:15; Luke 17:3; Ephesians 5:15; 1 Thessalonians 5:6

43

Helping Others

I pray that my grandchildren
will know the joy of generosity.

A Generous Spirit

Our daughter pulled into our driveway in their family van. Knowing that her three daughters were with her, Annie and I walked outside to say hello. When the door slid open, we both stuck our heads inside to greet our precious grandgirls. That's when my eye caught sight of a box on the floor containing what appeared to be individually wrapped granola bars, candy bars, boxed juices, packages of dried fruit, and a few other tasty items.

"Who's the stuff in the box for?" I asked. I can't tell you how warmed my heart was by the answer I got from the two older girls. I knew I was hearing the very essence of God's compassion as our granddaughters responded almost in unison:

> Oh, those are for the homeless people we meet. If we pull
> up beside someone at a red light or see them in a parking
> lot, they get one of the packages.

How proud I was of our daughter's deliberate effort at teaching her kids about generosity. I know the reality that in these times being generous and compassionate isn't a way of thinking that is commonly taught or fostered. Instead, people seem focused on making sure their own needs and wants are met first—then they might consider others.

Advertisers constantly stream ads on media that are more me-focused than other-focused. Do these quips sound familiar?

- Just do it!
- Obey your thirst!
- No boundaries!
- Got the urge?
- You deserve a break today!

These and a host of other slogans cater to the "me" in all of us. And as media bombard the airwaves, our grandchildren are especially vulnerable. Combating the onslaught of the advertising world's well-honed weaponry of words isn't easy, so I was impressed that our daughter was firing back by showing her children how to think of others and actively help. The "care packages" are an excellent tool that also benefit those in need.

I'm quite certain that Heidi's children won't forget the satisfaction that comes with giving. Because I want them to always consider others when it comes to generosity, I pray…

For My Grandchildren

Dear Father, I love how You instruct Your people to be compassionate and generous toward the poor and needy. In Your Word You taught the farmers to leave gleanings of their harvest for those who were hungry, and You commanded that the needy and poor were to be treated fairly. Your heart has always been open to their cries. Let my grandchildren show their gratitude for all they have by sharing with those who have less.

I want my grandchildren to be defenders of the oppressed. Guide them to go to the rescue of those in need, especially the weak and fatherless. You've warned us that the people who oppress the poor are showing contempt for their Maker, but

145

you affirm that the people who are kind to the destitute honor You. May my grandchildren be named among those who honor You by living with compassion and generosity. As they give to the poor, may their kindness be a gift to You.

Encourage my grandchildren to never shut their ears to the cries of the poor because when they cry out to You, O Lord, I want You to hear their cries. Fill my grandkids' hearts with compassion so they will never oppress the widow or the fatherless, the alien or the poor. All of us, both rich and poor, have this in common: You are the Maker of us all.

In Jesus' name, amen.

Leviticus 19:9-10; Deuteronomy 15:11; Psalm 82:3-4; Proverbs 14:31; Proverbs 19:17; Proverbs 21:13; Zechariah 7:10; Proverbs 22:2

44

Avoiding Addictions

I pray that my grandchildren
will avoid bad habits that can lead to
the stronghold of addiction.

Daddy Drank

As our grandchildren get older, I (Annie) want to let them know that a good way to not have to break an addiction is to not get involved with it in the first place. I can thankfully report to them that I've yet to try my first cigarette, taste my first beer, or take any kind of recreational drug. I will, of course, confess to them that it's not because I have super strength to resist and refuse these vices. In fact, there is another reason I choose to avoid them, and it's one that won't be so easy to reveal.

I have a propensity for addiction that is inherited. In my case, the looming culprit was alcohol. My father said to me one day, "I loved my dad, but there is no denying it. He was an alcoholic. And when he was drinking, he was a mean man." My dad went on to share, "Like him, I too developed a taste for liquor. I liked the smell of it. I liked how it made me feel. I liked everything about it. But there came a time when I had to make a choice. My father chose to spend his money to feed his addiction. I chose to use my money to feed my family."

It's hard to explain how deeply I admired and appreciated my dad's decision to avoid such a home-wrecking addiction that alcohol can be. I was also impressed with his openness. Both are main reasons why I consider him a great man. My sweet father was on Steve's mind when he and his friend Jeff Pearles wrote this song:

Daddy Drank

He was born in 1940; at eighteen took a wife
His calloused hands were plenty proof he worked
    hard all his life.
He fought for every penny, just to make ends meet.
And when worry got the best of him, he'd
    sneak off and drink.
In his secret place; at the throne of grace.

Daddy drank from the fountain of God's love.
Drowned his sorrows in that healing stream above.
On his knees we'd hear him crying when he prayed.
We give God thanks that our daddy drank.

Mama never had to wonder where he went to quench his thirst,
What he did on Saturday night never kept him out
    of Sunday church.
And we never had to be afraid when he came through the door.
He loved the taste of God's new wine—
    said he always needed more.
Kept him walkin' straight
On the narrow way.

This old world could use a lot more men
Who know how to drink like him.

Yes, Daddy drank from the fountain of God's love.
Drowned his sorrows in that healing stream above.
On his knees we'd hear him crying when he prayed.
We give God thanks that our daddy drank.[16]

I know there are many destructive addictions my grandkids need to avoid. As time goes on, in case they're tempted, I will continue to pray…

For My Grandchildren

Heavenly Father, please shield my grandchildren and protect them from the cruel taskmaster that addiction can be. I ask You to be their stronghold…their strong tower and place of refuge in times of trouble. When temptation comes, step in and remind them that You are their best source of relief from the stresses of this life. Let them know that in You only will they find peace of mind. I long for them to find their safe haven in You instead of in any ungodly activity or mind-altering substance.

Open their eyes to see that though they walk in the flesh, they don't war according to the flesh. You've provided the weapons necessary to win the war over addictions and bad habits. But the weapons they fight with aren't carnal. It is through Your Spirit and in Your power that evil strongholds are defeated.

Give my grandchildren the courage to cast down arguments and every high thing that exalts itself against the knowledge of You. Through Your powerful Holy Spirit, I pray they will bring every thought into captivity to the obedience of Christ.

Deliver them in times of enticement. Your Word gives the assurance that there is no temptation that can overtake them. You, O God, are faithful and will not let them be tempted beyond their ability, but with the temptation, You will also provide a way of escape, that they may be able to endure it.

Remind my grandchildren that their bodies are temples of the Holy Spirit, who lives inside them. They are not their own, but they've been bought with a price. Father, help them to honor You with their bodies by keeping them as a holy temple where You live. Help them not make their bodies garbage dumps for things and thoughts that could lead to bad habits and addictions.

In Jesus' name, amen.

Psalm 18:2; 2 Corinthians 10:3-5; Psalm 9:9;
1 Corinthians 10:13; 1 Corinthians 6:19-20

45

Navigating Life's Seas

I pray that my grandchildren
will never let someone else's bad behavior
change who they are.

Keeping the Boat Afloat

Using an illustration of a small rowboat, I (Annie) was able to help our grandchildren understand what happens when we let someone else's behavior change the way we act. I explained that a boat can float on the deepest ocean and not sink. Regardless of the enormous amount of water that surrounds it, it can bob along unaffected. Not until its hull has been breached, which allows water inside, will there be any danger to the boat or those in it. Sadly enough, I had a personal story to share with them that highlighted this truth.

Early one morning, I drove to a local store to pick up a few last-minute items in preparation for company we were having that afternoon. In my haste to leave the house, I forgot to get my grocery list. As I pulled into the parking lot, I was a bit distracted with trying to remember all the items I had to buy. I started to pull into the very first row of parking spaces. However, I noticed that not many cars were in the lot at such an early hour, so at the last second I decided to drive a few rows over so I would be closer to the grocery section.

As I made the unexpected swerve back into the driving lane, I noticed in my peripheral vision a car passing that had to jog just a bit because of my driving. I could see the woman driver was going totally bonkers. I braked and waited for her to pass. While window to window with her, I watched as she very angrily made gestures with her flailing hands and contorted her body in such a way that clearly displayed her impatience with my indecision.

I couldn't believe it! This woman was having a fit over something so small and unimportant as my changing my mind about where I was going to park. There was never a danger of us colliding. I glared at the irrational woman. Her belligerence was shocking to me, but not half as shocking as the response I offered. Without thinking it through for even a millisecond, I did the first thing that came to my befuddled mind. I stuck my tongue out at her! Yep. I found myself acting as irrational as she was.

When the stranger saw my tongue sticking out of my mouth like an anteater at an anthill, she really lost it. It wasn't until that moment I noticed she was a large woman with fiery rage shooting out of her eyes. For the sake of survival, I decided I'd better hightail it out of there and go to another store.

What happened to me that day? I know what I was feeling, but what was I thinking? Yes, the other woman was acting very juvenile (in my opinion), but there was no reason I should have allowed her behavior to affect me in such an immature way.

Needless to say, my grandkids were quite surprised that their normally levelheaded grandmother reacted in such a childish way. I carefully explained to them that I was very much in the wrong. I told them that on that particular day I let my little boat sink to the bottom of the "Sea of Bad Behavior."

I hope my confession will help them avoid the same mistake. Just in case, I pray…

For My Grandchildren

Dear Father, help my grandchildren keep their behavior righteous in You. Show them that they don't have to let another person's bad behavior change them into people You don't want them to be. Help them resist the temptation to repay evil for evil. Instead show them what is right in Your eyes. As much as it depends on my grandchildren, help them to live at peace with everyone. I pray they will not take revenge on those who have done them wrong, but will leave room for You to do Your work. You let us know clearly in Your Word that *You* are the only One who has room to judge and avenge a wrong.

Keep my grandchildren's boats afloat despite the tumult of evil around them. Please give them the strength to overcome evil with good.

I pray that in this day and age, my grandchildren will be Your bright lights shining in the darkness. Darkness can't extinguish Your light; Your light makes the darkness flee. Remind my grandchildren to not repay those who insult them by returning an insult. Instead, encourage them to repay them with blessings because my grandchildren were called for this purpose so they might inherit a blessing.

Dear Lord, reveal to my grandchildren how they can love their neighbors…and love their enemies. Help them pray for those who persecute them. For in this they will demonstrate the perfecting work You are doing in their lives. May their choice to react in love no matter how they're being treated bring glory to You.

In Jesus' name, amen.

Romans 12:17-18; Romans 12:19-21; 1 John 1:5; 1 Peter 3:8-12; Matthew 5:43-48

46

Saying No to Sex

I pray that my grandsons
will stay morally pure.

"List of Fools"

If I live long enough to be around when my grandson is old enough to ask, "Grandpa, do you have any advice for me about girls?" I have a plan. If my fingers still work and I still have a voice, I'll break out my old Gibson guitar and sing the following song that was written more than 30 years before he was born.

List of Fools

I was standing at my window when I saw a young man,
Walking late at night near her corner.
He was old enough to be there, but too young to understand
The sorrow he had found when he met her.

She was dressed like a harlot, she had evil on her mind.
Not looking for a lover—just a victim.
And with her words she flattered him,
    and it scattered his good sense.
I knew that boy was caught when she kissed him.

And tonight she will add him to her long list of fools
And leave him to suffer in his wounds.
Her pleasure for a moment will give him years of pain…
To know his name is on a harlot's list of fools.

Oh, you young men, won't you listen to some wisdom…
Don't you get caught in her ways.
'Cause her house is on the highway that will lead you to your
    grave.
Don't let her take you astray.

'Cause if you do she'll just add you to her long list of fools
And leave you to suffer in your wounds.
Her pleasure for a moment will give you years of pain…
To know your name is on a harlot's list of fools.[17]

I'm confident that if my grandson can endure my not-so-modern style of music, and if he heeds the warning in the lyric, my little song can help him avoid a ton of spiritual and emotional trouble when it comes to temptations involving females. Why do I feel so sure? Is it because it's a story his old granddad concocted? Nope. It's because the lyric is a condensed paraphrase of Proverbs 7:6-27, and God's Word is packed with powerful, life-changing wisdom.

Included in the categories of subjects God addresses in His Word is the issue of moral purity. Through the Scriptures my grandson can know what constitutes good moral values, how to develop them, how to keep them, and how to regain purity if it's been lost. For example, in the Proverbs story about the harlot, the young man's first mistake was going where women like her were known to hang out. Second, it would have been good for him to recognize the attire of a harlot, and that "a boisterous woman" is often masking rebellion. She's the kind he should have walked away from the moment he saw her. Third, if he'd known that a harlot's bait bucket is stocked with items she knows can lure a victim, he could have avoided being snagged on her hook. A kiss, flattering lips, a little bit of religion thrown in for the boy whose conscience might be trying to speak ("I was due to offer peace offerings; today I have paid my vows," Proverbs 7:14) are just a few of her enticements.

The lessons to be learned from this pitiful young man caught by the harlot are numerous. But if my grandson will hear me, we'll go through them when he asks that type of question. Until then, in regard to how he relates to girls, I will pray...

For My Grandson

O Father in heaven, thank You for all the guidance You provide in Your written Word to help my grandson be wise when it comes to how he relates to girls and women. I know it's Your will that he should be sanctified, that he should avoid sexual immorality, and that he should learn to control his own body in a way that is holy and honorable to You. Please help him not incite passionate lust in himself or others. Protect him so he'll never take advantage of a girl or woman. I pray this because You warn that You will punish all those who commit such sins. Let my grandson hear and respond to Your command not to be impure, but to live a holy life. Impress on his heart that if he rejects this instruction he will not be rejecting just his dad, or me, or any other human being, but he'll be rejecting You, the very One who gave him the Holy Spirit.

Teach my grandson that his body wasn't made for sexual immorality; it was made for You. I know that his hormones will create incredibly strong desires, so I ask that You encourage him to turn to You as the answer to his deepest longings. Teach him that his body is part of Christ Himself. I don't want my grandson to take any part of Christ and join Him to a prostitute or other immoral person or act. Help him know that the one who is united with You is one with You in spirit.

Guide my grandson so he'll be discerning when it comes to women, that he will recognize evil intent when he sees it whether in the flesh, on a computer or TV screen, or in the pages of a book or magazine. When he does recognize it, help him flee youthful lusts—but not just run from it but that he would in his heart run toward You. You are his only source of strength and righteousness. Give him like-minded friends who hold to Your standards, who call on You with pure hearts, who share Your strength and wisdom so they can encourage each other to maintain purity. I pray too that You will help my grandson be a blessing to others in the ways they are blessings to him.

Because I know it's possible to fail in these areas, please teach my grandson that if he sins he has an Advocate with You. That Advocate is Jesus Christ the righteous, who provided payment for the sins of us all through the sacrifice He made at Calvary. Blessed be Your name, Lord, for showing such understanding forgiveness. May my grandson choose to embrace Your grace whenever he fails.

Father, please be with the young lady who will eventually become my grandson's bride. Guide her in purity. Give her the strength to avoid the deadly mistakes of promiscuity and sexual immorality. Protect her from the evil one. Lead her safely, both physically and spiritually, through the days that will carry her to my grandson's side. Even now bless their union.

All these things I ask in Christ's mighty, powerful, and pure name, amen.

1 Thessalonians 4:3-8; 1 Corinthians 6:12-20; 2 Timothy 2:22; 1 John 2:1

47

Doing God's Will

*I pray that my grandchildren
will know and do the will of God.*

The Two Missing Parts

If I (Steve) live long enough to see my grandchildren grow into their late teens and face the nerve-testing challenges that come with impending adulthood, and if they ask me what's most important to remember as they do, I'm ready to respond. My reply will include a story about a weed-eater engine I had to repair...

> I had a weed eater that wasn't running right so I disassembled the engine, cleaned the carburetor, replaced the spark plug and fuel filter, got it all back together, and tried to start it. It turned over fine, but it just wouldn't fire up. After nearly ruining my shoulder by yanking the start rope and getting nothing out of the engine, I was ready to throw it into the trash dump.
>
> Then I saw the problem. There on the workbench I saw two very important parts I'd forgotten to include when reassembling the motor: a little spring that goes in the carburetor and the screw that holds it in. When I got those two parts installed, I yanked the starter rope again. Bingo! The engine fired up.

After I tell them the weed-eater engine story I'll add, "If you ever come to a time in life when things aren't running right, consider the possibility that you have two parts missing. Without them nothing works well. Those two parts are 1) to *know* the will of God, and 2) to *do* the will of God. Until that day comes when I have the opportunity to share this story, I will pray…

For My Grandchildren

Heavenly Father, I bring my grandchildren to Your throne and ask that You daily reveal to them that for everything to run right in their lives they need to know Your will and do all they can to follow it.

There are many things I don't know, but I know for sure that You desire all people to be saved and to come to a knowledge of the truth. You've revealed that it's not Your will that any should perish, but that all should come to repentance before You and seek Your saving grace. Therefore, I'm confident that it's within Your will that I pray for the salvation of my grandchildren. Please save them. Please help them understand and accept the sacrifice of Your Son on the cross for their sins.

After they come to know You, encourage their spiritual growth. I want them to mature in their faith. I ask that You help them to do their best to present themselves to You as people approved, workers who do not need to be ashamed and who correctly handle the Word of truth.

I pray they'll present their bodies as living, holy sacrifices to You. There's no doubt that this would be pleasing to You. It's a spiritual act of worship. And, Father, I earnestly pray they will not conform to this world system, but they will let You change how they think by renewing their minds.

Open my grandchildren's hearts so they'll allow the Holy Spirit to strengthen them, lead them, and intercede for them. As my Lord and Savior prayed in the Garden, "Not my will, but yours be done," please give my grandchildren the courage and desire to pray likewise.

Give them the desire to make the best of choices by always being willing to follow Your Word and follow the light You give them. I pray they will keep themselves from all forms of immoral behavior and useless activities. I want them to inherit Your kingdom. Wash them and sanctify them with Your Word and by Your blood, Jesus. When they cry out to You, answer them in a way they can hear and understand.

O good Shepherd, I so want my grandchildren to know You. I desire that they will instantly recognize and listen to Your voice. I pray they'll be confident that to know and do Your will is to love mercy and to walk humbly with You.

I know You're at work all around us. Let my grandchildren recognize what You're doing and quickly and joyfully join You in Your work. If they do, they will always be in the center of Your will.

In Jesus' name, amen.

1 Timothy 2:3-4; Luke 19:10; Ephesians 2:5; 2 Timothy 2:15; Romans 12:1-2; Romans 8:26-27; Luke 22:42; 1 Corinthians 6:9-11; John 10:14; Micah 6:8

48

Using Time Wisely

I pray that my grandchildren
will use their time wisely.

Ticks of the Clock

When it comes to the ticking of the clock, our economic situation, our physical characteristics, the shades of our complexions, or where we live has no bearing. Each of us is granted 86,400 seconds each day (if you feel you need more time, go with 31,557,600 seconds per year). While the amount of time we're given is an important detail, what we do with it is of greater significance in terms of the impact on our lives as well as the lives of those around us. For example, we can waste our time playing video games or we can bake a cake and take it to the family across the street that lost a loved one. We can write a slanderous social media posting or we can write a letter to encourage a young pastor who is discouraged and wants to give up on the call on his life. The amount of time used is basically the same, but obviously there are profoundly different impacts.

Oh, how I (Annie) long for my grandchildren to come to an understanding of how incredibly important it is that they wisely use every moment, second, minute, hour, day, week, month, and year they're given in a positive manner. The implications aren't just temporal— they're eternal too. It's for this reason I pray...

For My Grandchildren

Dear Lord, in the time You've assigned to my grandchildren, I pray they will use it to build up people, not tear them down. I ask that You help them to live their lives well—not as unwise but as wise believers in You, making the most of their days. Show them that the time they do have, if not used in accordance to Your will, might yield temptations and self-destruction.

Help them exercise wisdom in regard to the time spent interacting with others. May they make the most of each and every opportunity that comes to them to do something redeemable. As they commit their ways to You, please bless their efforts and make their plans succeed.

Guide my grandchildren so they'll choose to use their time to establish, develop, and maintain good relationships with family and friends rather than squandering their days in the pursuit of material treasures that won't last or fully satisfy. I pray that by the end of their lives, they'll have more to show than a bunch of possessions that become a smorgasbord for moths and rust and a magnet for thieves to break in and steal. I pray that when their time is spent, they'll not have regrets and heartaches as they evaluate how their time was invested or, worse, how it was wasted.

Please show them, dear Father, that they have a finite amount of time to fulfill Your purpose; their days are numbered and their lives are fleeting gifts from You. You've made their days the size of a hand, yet You've declared that the days You've provided for them are enough.

Let my grandchildren be diligent and use their time wisely. I don't want them to be sluggards who crave everything and get nothing. Each morning when they awaken to a new day, remind them to redeem their time by using it for Your glory.

You've told us that our days will be seventy years, maybe eighty if we're healthy. When I was young that sounded like a long time, yet now, even with all the troubles and sorrows that come with life, the years seem to pass quickly and soon I'll fly away. Lord, I want to use my time to pray for my grandchildren. And if I'm blessed by You and granted additional days, please encourage me to remain faithful to pray for my children, grandchildren, and great-grandchildren.

I know there is nothing I can do to change my ancestors, but through prayer I can influence the direction and destiny of my descendants. Give me the strength to show the same diligence to the end in order to make Your hope sure in the lives of my extended family. I don't want to be lazy! Help me imitate those who, through faith and patience, inherit what You've promised.

In Jesus' name, amen.

Ephesians 5:15-16; Colossians 4:5; Matthew 6:19; Psalm 39:4-5; Proverbs 13:4; Psalm 90:10; Psalm 33:11; Hebrews 6:11-12

49

Celebrating God and Making Memories

I pray that my grandchildren will have good memories of their grandparents.

Memory Makers

Steve and I have an advantage regarding our roles as grandparents that some of our co-grandparents don't enjoy. We're blessed to live less than an hour from all of our grandkids. We consider the 35 miles between us to be nothing compared to some grandparents we know who have to go to the other side of the world to see their grands. Of course, our closeness has challenges that go with it.

Because we're nearby and we get to see them often, the amount of energy expended during their frequent visits, especially extended ones, is significant. Though it can be taxing, we've found a solution to the physical drain. Basically, after a full day or an overnight stay, and especially after a multiday visit, we wave goodbye as we watch them leave with their parents, and then we get into our car and drive to the hospital where we both get blood transfusions. Well, not really, but we've thought about it.

In regard to how tiring childcare can be for us "older folks," our hearts go out to those who aren't just grandparenting, but they're also parenting their grandkids. Whether their reentry into parenthood is due to the death of the parents, divorce, or other serious problems, raising kids is definitely a tough job generally designed for younger people.

Being parents during our younger years takes an immense physical and mental toll on us; doing it all again when we're older requires a level of effort that is hard for me to imagine. The grandparents we know who are currently in the throes of raising their grandkids have our admiration as well as our prayers for their stamina.

While Steve and I are more than willing to step in and parent our grandkids if needed, how grateful we are right now to focus on being grandparents. As I see it, at this time Steve and I have one clearly defined job as granddad and grandma—to be memory makers. We recognize that their parents have the greater, more significant, and multi-layered job of providing for all of their children's necessary needs, such as educating them, correcting them, developing their characters, and leaving legacies for them to follow. Our job as grandparents isn't complicated. We're given the pleasurable task of doing things that fill the scrapbooks in their hearts with mental photos that remind them of time spent with us and what we believe in.

How do we fill their hearts with good memories of us (and fulfill our goal of making sure they miss us when we're gone)? Here are just three things in our toolbox of memory-making opportunities:

- We provide an enjoyable place for them to come and visit. There are bicycles, tricycles, and Big Wheels in our garage (purchased at garage sales). We have a corner in our sunroom filled with toys and art supplies. And there's an Amish-built playhouse and swing set in the backyard (something our own kids never had growing up).

- In addition to the "playland" we've created at our house, we take them to fun, educational places that their parents struggle to find time to do. There are museums, concerts, child-centered events, ball games, shopping centers, garage sales (one of their favorite activities), and many other places to go with them.

- And we make sure we always have stashes of ice-cream treats and popcorn.

We admit that creating lasting memories in the minds and hearts of our grandkids is an energy (and cash) consuming responsibility. Still, we think it's worth every calorie burned and dollar spent. While we actually have a lot of fun, we take these pleasurable tasks very seriously. We often pray...

For Our Grandchildren

Dear Father in heaven, help us as grandparents create an environment in our hearts and in our home where our children's children will always feel welcome, safe, and spiritually blessed. Our greatest desire as Grandma and Grandpa is that You'll help us help them see You in us and the world around them. If we fail to leave them the inheritance of faith in their memory of us, we'll be sorely disappointed. Please help us show the next generation how to sing praises of You—You, Your strength, and Your wonderful works.

We also long to provide a place where good memories are made...the kind that will last all their days even until their time comes when they become grandparents. In that day, if they look back and say, "I want to be a grandparent like my grandma and grandpa were for me," we'll know we did our jobs right...and we'll have You to thank for it.

In Christ's name, amen.

John 17:6; Proverbs 13:22; Psalm 78:1-4

50

Finishing Well

I pray that my grandchildren
will finish their race with
their light still shining.

Music City "Half Mom-a-thon"

After months of training on the hilly streets of Nashville and putting countless miles on her "go nowhere" treadmill in her upstairs den, the day finally came for our daughter, Heidi, to run her first long race. She chose the Music City Half Marathon challenge. Because I planned to take two of her girls to the race to see their mother run by, I called it "The Music City Half Mom-a-thon."

The Saturday morning of the race arrived with a sky filled with ominous clouds. The local TV station reported that the weather wasn't expected to favor the more than 10,000 runners gathered for the race. Sure enough, the rain started early and didn't stop throughout the duration of the event. Because of the downpour, I didn't take Heidi's oldest two girls to the race early. Our goal was to see Heidi run by the eight-mile marker.

To shield herself from the steady rainfall and be able to endure the chill, Heidi found a clear plastic trash bag to put on over her running gear. We didn't know about her added attire as we stood on the corner in the rain that had turned torrential. We watched for our beloved runner, but due to the blinding rain and the numbers of people who were covered with plastic and looked the same as they ran by, we never did catch sight of Heidi.

The good news is that Heidi finished the race. It was a major accomplishment for her to have completed such a demanding challenge. We were so proud of her for setting such a lofty goal and attaining it. While my granddaughters wished they'd been able to spot their mom out on the course, they weren't disappointed with the outcome.

I've thought many times about Heidi's feat of endurance at the "Mom-a-thon." When I do, I'm inspired to consider the race of life. Just as Heidi crossed the line with joy regardless of the hindering rain, I too want to finish the course that is set before me. And I want to do it well. I don't wish this for just me, though. I wish to succeed for my grandchildren too.

To help the girls appreciate the spiritual insights that can be gleaned from running a long race, I shared with them the difference between the race their mother ran and a marathon in ancient days. Unlike these days when the winner is the one who crosses the finish line first, back then the prize didn't always go to the first one across the line. Instead, it went to the runner who crossed the line first—*with the torch he carried still lit.*

Heidi's girls understood that if the race their mother finished was held in days of old, no one would have been the winner because the rain would have doused every torch. In spiritual terms, however, as we run the race of life with the light of Christ burning in our hearts no amount of rain, wind, or anything else can extinguish the flame of His love. Because of that, we can run our race with confidence, knowing that when we cross the line we will be winners.

Steve wrote a song that contains a chorus that has become our theme song. We've taught it to our grandkids too. Even though the words are targeted toward an older crowd, they're very applicable to young people. We hope this becomes the cry of their hearts.

> I want to finish well.
> I want to end this race
> Still leaning on His amazing grace.
> I want my last few miles to testify
> That God never fails.

I don't want to fall down this close to the line.
I want to finish well.[18]

With this as my hope, I earnestly pray…

For My Grandchildren

Dear Father, I know there is a finish line in everyone's race. When I think about my grandchildren, my sincere prayer is that I won't be alive to see them cross theirs. Hopefully, I'll have finished my race and will be standing in the great cloud of witnesses cheering them on from the balcony of heaven. But while I'm here, I ask You to help my grandchildren lay aside every encumbrance and every sin that easily entangles them so they can run their races with endurance. I want them to fix their eyes on Jesus, the author and perfecter of their faith. I pray they will not grow weary and lose heart when the road gets rough and obstacles are in their paths.

Encourage them to finish their races and complete their tasks the Lord Jesus has given them—the task of testifying to the good news of Your grace.

Give my grandchildren wisdom so they'll understand that in a regular race all the runners run, but only one gets the prize. I pray they will run their races of life in such a way as to get the prize of an everlasting crown given by You. I long for my grandchildren to hear You say at the end of their races, "Well done, good and faithful servants."

In Jesus' name, amen.

Hebrews 12:1-3; Acts 20:24; 1 Corinthians 9:23-25;
Matthew 25:21

51

Enduring Faith

I pray for my grandchildren's parents
as they prepare their children for the future.

"Get 'Em Ready!"

As I (Steve) watch our young grandchildren running in our yard, riding bicycles up and down our driveway, or sleeping in the bunk beds upstairs, sometimes my emotions swing from one extreme to another. In one moment I'm deeply warmed by how carefree our grandkids are, how sweet and unique their flowering personalities are, and how fun their innocent and often humorous antics are to enjoy. In the next moment I feel a sadness caused by the darkening cloud of godlessness that is over our nation, even our world. The perilous time we live in is a burden their very young shoulders have yet to carry, and at their ages that's a good thing. But I know their parents feel the weight of the uncertain times we're in and are proactively doing something about it.

I'm blessed beyond description by knowing our grandchildren are daily hearing Bible stories in their homes, learning life-changing biblical concepts through carefully chosen media tools, and receiving weekly opportunities to learn the value of fellowship at church. I'm grateful to report that our children and their spouses are doing an incredible job raising our grandkids in the admonition of the Lord. In response to their timely actions, I wrote the following lyric to inspire other young parents to do the same.

"Get 'Em Ready!"

Get 'em ready for the times ahead.
Fill the hearts of your children with the words in red.
It'll feed their souls when a bag of gold won't buy
    a loaf of bread.
Get 'em ready for the times ahead.

Get 'em ready, for the days to come
When they'll have to march alone to the sound
    of the angel's drums.
If they're gonna stand for truth, it'll be up to you to
    show them how it's done.
Get 'em ready for the days to come.

Take a look into your children's eyes.
Do you see the shadows of the night
Falling 'cross this land we love?
Their only hope is in the blood...
    to be covered by the blood.

Get 'em ready for the hour is near,
When a voice will come from heaven only the
    redeemed will hear.
He's gonna call us away and, on that day, will they
    be among the ones who disappear?
Get 'em ready for the hour is near.

They're gonna need faith, they're gonna need grace
To face what they're gonna go through.
Get 'em ready—that's what love would do.[19]

    As our children and their spouses continue to prepare our grand-children for the future, Annie and I will do what we can to contribute to their efforts. Of all the ways we can help, I know the most powerful thing we can do is pray...

For My Grandchildren

Father in heaven, the days we're living in seem to resemble the days of Noah. So many people are going about their business without much concern that a flood of judgment is coming. How thankful I am that our grandchildren live in homes where their parents are aware of the clouds of irreverence, immorality, and wickedness that have not only moved in but seem to be welcomed—even celebrated—by the masses.

I pray that our children will continue to honor Christ the Lord as holy, and that they're prepared to defend the hope that is in them. Help them teach their children to do the same. May our children stay spiritually awake at all times and remain prayerful. Give them and their children the strength to escape the things of evil that will take place on the earth.

Lord, I know that in this world there will be tribulation, but let our children be of good cheer because You've already overcome the world. As they face the storms of unrest that hover over the world, may they and their children find rest in the shadow of Your mighty presence.

Guide our children as they lead our grandkids to You and a deeper faith in Your promises. I know if they endure to the end, they'll be saved in You. I ask this to Your glory alone.

In Christ's name, amen.

Matthew 24:37-39; Romans 2:5-11; 1 Peter 3:15; Luke 21:36; John 16:33; Psalm 91:1; Matthew 24:13

52

Praying for Them

God, please do for our grandchildren what
You've graciously done for many others
who have trusted You throughout history.

A Benediction

Together we've offered a lot of prayers to God for our grandkids. We hope you've found them meaningful, and that your confidence in the Lord's willingness to hear and answer them has been strengthened because they were based on God's Word. We encourage you to return to these prayers often. Read them aloud with trust, hope, and praise.

Hopefully you've also been inspired to write down your own prayers for your grandchildren. What a beautiful testament it would be to them when they're old enough to understand your dedication to praying on their behalf.

As one final suggestion, we offer the following song lyric to you to be used as a blessing for your grandchildren. It was written with my friend Lindsey Williams, who brought the idea to a songwriting session not long after he and his wife waved farewell to their son, who was making his first flight from their nest to land on a college campus several hours away.

Like the Williams' house that grew eerily quiet and the chair at their dinner table that remained unused, someday the rooms in our homes will grow quiet again. The area around our kitchen tables will no longer be spattered with bits of banana, cereal remnants, and bread crumbs. The toys that tripped us will be put away. This happens because, like our kids did, our grandchildren's world will expand and the time they spend with us will diminish.

Right now when we can still hold them, sometimes Annie and I put our hands on their heads or on their backs and silently sing the blessing contained in these lyrics.

This Is My Prayer

We've come a long way together
Down this road of life.
Now it's time for you to leave—
It's your turn to fly.
Now every hope and dream I have for you
    will follow you everywhere.
This is my prayer…

I pray God will remember you like Noah in the flood,
And favor you like Moses, with power from above.
Fight for you like Israel when they marched 'round Jericho,
And every wall you face will fall down and,
    you'll take the higher ground.
That's what I pray for you.

You're gonna climb many mountains;
You'll have some valleys low.
It won't matter where you are
Or how far you go.
As long as I have a breath to breathe,
    my heart'll be with you there.
This is my prayer.

I pray God will protect you like Daniel in the lions' den.
You'll sing a song of salvation just like Miriam did.
And faith for you like Peter had when he stepped
    out of the boat,
And if you ever start sinking down you'll see
    the Lord reaching out.
That's what I pray for you.

And that He'll use you like Paul,
Anoint you like King David,
Honor you like Mary.
This is what I'm praying…

I pray God will remember you like Noah in the flood,
And favor you like Moses, with power from above.
And fight for you like Israel when they
    marched 'round Jericho,
And every wall you face will fall down, and
    you'll take the higher ground.
That's what I pray for you.[20]

⌒♾

The LORD bless you and keep you;
the LORD make His face shine upon you,
and be gracious to you; the LORD lift up His countenance
upon you, and give you peace.
Numbers 6:24-26

Lyric Credits